ABOVE THE SHOULDERS

MASTER THE MIND THAT MAKES THE
IMPOSSIBLE INEVITABLE

JASON NACEY

Cover design by Marden Blake – www.from3838.com

First Edition – May 2025
ISBN: 979-8-9986174-0-9
U.S. Copyright Registration Number: TXu 2-483-679

Published by
DangerNacey Publishing
www.abovetheshoulders.com

First and foremost, to my incredible wife—your unwavering support through every 4 AM alarm, every finish line, and every moment of doubt has been my foundation. You never questioned if I could, only how I would, and that belief carried me through more than you know.

To my children—whether joining me for tire flips in the backyard, cheering at race courses, or waiting at finish lines with those unforgettable smiles— you've taught me that true strength isn't just about personal achievement but the example we set for those watching. You make every challenge worthwhile.

To Brian—your friendship has been a masterclass in the power of the right circle. Your consistent encouragement pushed me beyond comfortable limitations, your honest feedback sharpened my thinking, and your belief in me often exceeded my own. This book, like so many of my greatest achievements, bears your invisible signature.

I'm grateful to Alex Ferreira, Ashley Caldwell, Alex Kopacz, Sam Pedlow, and Yura Min for generously allowing me to share their inspiring stories.

And to everyone who has been part of my journey—training partners, mentors, competitors, friends & family—thank you for playing your role in this ongoing story of growth, challenge, and discovery that happens above the shoulders.

CONTENTS

Foreword   vii

Introduction   xi

PART I
THE MIND—THE FOUNDATION OF EVERYTHING

Chapter 1: Resilience—Your Inner Superpower   3

Chapter 2: The Forge of the Mind   22

Chapter 3: Mindset—The Only Thing You Can Control   35

Chapter 4: The Stories We Tell Ourselves—Are You Setting Yourself Up to Win or Lose?   58

Chapter 5: The Secret to Beating Negative Thought Loops   78

PART II
TRAINING YOUR MIND FOR SUCCESS (HOWEVER YOU DEFINE IT)

Chapter 6: The Science of Goal-Setting and Mental Focus   97

Chapter 7: The Champion Mindset—How Champions Are Made   112

Chapter 8: Building 'Never Quit' Into Your DNA   141

Chapter 9: The Gratitude Hack: A Mental Weapon for Resilience   165

PART III
ADAPTING, GROWING, AND THRIVING

Chapter 10: How to Handle Change and Uncertainty Like a Pro   181

Chapter 11: The Power of Habits—Your Brain's Shortcut to Success   195

PART IV
SHAPING YOUR LIFE THROUGH MINDSET

Chapter 12: The People Around You Determine Your Success   211

Chapter 13: Lifelong Growth—How to Keep Expanding Your Potential   224

Pull the Trigger: Your 90-Day Plan   237

Index   241
About the Author   244

FOREWORD

I remember standing at the finish line of a Death Race in Vermont, watching a Wall Street executive I'd pushed beyond breaking point for 60 hours straight. When he finally crossed that line—feet bloody, hands raw—he didn't celebrate. He looked me dead in the eyes and said, "That wasn't about the race. That was about killing the person I was before." That transformation is what Spartan has always been about.

I've spent my life dragging people out of their comfort zones—sometimes kicking and screaming—because I've learned the hard truth: nothing worth having comes easy. When Jason sent me his manuscript, I recognized immediately what he was building. Not just another book about mental toughness, but a battle plan for rewiring how people approach every challenge in their lives.

The fitness industry sells shortcuts. The self-help world peddles feel-good platitudes. What sets Jason's work apart is its unflinching honesty about what actually transforms people: the daily, unglamorous work of mental conditioning that happens when no one's watching. The kind that doesn't fit in an Instagram post but builds the foundation for everything that matters.

On Spartan courses worldwide, I've watched thousands of competitors hit their breaking point. The ones who finish aren't always the strongest or fastest—they're the ones who've trained their minds to reject surrender as an option. During my decades building this global movement, I've discovered what Jason articulates perfectly in these pages: physical challenges are merely the arena where mental mastery reveals itself.

The parallels between Jason's *Mental Mastery Pyramid* and what we've built at Spartan are striking. His focus on incremental challenges, creating systems over relying on motivation, and building the right support network mirrors exactly what separates finishers from DNFs in the toughest races we've designed.

I've watched my own children learn these lessons on our courses, just as Jason describes his son's transformation in the Abu Dhabi desert. These aren't just races—they're laboratories for developing the grit that carries over into everything else. His frameworks give names to what I've observed empirically: that mindset is trainable, resilience is buildable, and mental toughness is the ultimate competitive advantage in a world where too many quit at the first sign of discomfort.

I've seen people transform their entire lives by mastering what happens between their ears. Whether it's conquering physical challenges, building businesses from nothing, or developing unshakable confidence in any situation—the battle always begins in the mind. After decades of watching millions cross Spartan finish lines, I've noticed winners share one trait: they don't wait for the perfect moment or permission to begin. They make decisions, take immediate action, and deliberately surround themselves with people who hold them to higher standards. Jason's book gives you the exact blueprint to join their ranks.

Don't read these pages passively. Attack them like an obstacle. Apply them immediately. The principles Jason lays out aren't just theories —they're battle-tested tools forged in real struggle. I've built my life and business on the belief that humans are capable of 20x more than they think possible. This book gives you the mental framework to prove me right.

- Joe De Sena
Founder and CEO, Spartan Race

INTRODUCTION

Above the Shoulders: Unlock the Mind That Makes the Impossible Inevitable

Imagine standing at the edge of everything you've ever wanted—a dream so big it terrifies you. That marathon finish line. The business that keeps you up at night. Walking into any room and owning it without a flicker of doubt. It's right there, just beyond your fingertips, calling your name.

But something's blocking you, and it's not your body, your bank account, or the hand life dealt you. It's not even the world saying "no." It's a whisper in your mind, quiet but relentless: *You're not enough.* And you've been listening.

What if that voice is lying? What if the real you—the one capable of shattering limits, rewriting rules, and turning dreams into done deals —is already there, waiting just above your shoulders? What if everything you've ever wanted hinges not on what you lack, but on what you choose to believe?

This isn't just a book. It's a wake-up call. A map to the hidden superpower you've carried all along: your mind. *Above the Shoulders* isn't about fleeting pep talks or feel-good fluff—it's a gritty, hands-on guide to forging a mental edge so sharp it cuts through fear, doubt, and every excuse you've ever made. Because here's the truth I've lived, bled, and battled to learn: life is 90% above the shoulders. Master that, and the other 10% falls into place.

The Day I Saw the Truth

This revelation didn't come to me in a flash of insight—it emerged through years of struggle, failure, and eventual breakthrough. It began when my dad told me, "Sports are 80% above the shoulders." It was a passing comment that lodged in my memory but took years to truly understand. Back then, I brushed it off. I was busy chasing the game, collecting more bruises than victories, convinced that winning came from muscle, hustle, or luck—until life crushed that belief.

It hit me first on a wrestling mat. Down on points, lungs burning, opponent dominating—that moment when everything in you wants to concede defeat. Then something shifted above my shoulders that changed everything—a mental switch that transformed not just that match, but my entire understanding of human potential. That wrestling mat became my first proving ground for what I now call the 90% principle—a mindset shift that's echoed throughout every transformation I've experienced since.

I confirmed it during the Spartan Beast World Championship, my legs seizing under a merciless desert sun. My body screamed stop. My mind said one more step. One more step became the finish line.

I etched it into my bones during an Ironman, 140.6 miles of proof that limits are just stories we tell ourselves.

Dad was wrong. It's not 80%. It's 90%. Everything—resilience, success, the life you actually want—begins between your ears.

This 90% principle isn't just a catchy phrase—it's the foundation of what I call the *Mental Mastery Pyramid*. At its base lies resilience, the ability to withstand any challenge. Above that sits your internal narrative, the stories that either propel or sabotage you. Then comes focused execution, followed by perspective-shifting gratitude. At the pyramid's peak is the champion's mindset—the culmination of all these elements working in harmony.

I've witnessed this pyramid transform not just my own journey—from a guy who couldn't swim 25 yards without gasping for air to an Ironman finisher—but also those closest to me. Most powerfully, I saw it in my son's eyes after we completed the Spartan Beast World Championship together. Standing atop that desert mountain that had nearly broken both of us, his face streaked with dirt and sweat, I watched him transform from a kid into a warrior who understood that mental strength outlasts physical limits. Throughout this book, we'll build this pyramid level by level, with each chapter adding a crucial component to your mental arsenal.

Your Invitation to the Edge

Close your eyes for a second. Picture that one thing you've convinced yourself is impossible. The marathon. The business. The bold, unapologetic you you've always wanted to be. See it vividly—feel the sweat, hear the cheers, taste the victory. Write it down. Right now. That's your impossible goal, your North Star for this journey. Hold onto this. We'll come back to it throughout our journey together, and by the end, you'll see it through entirely new eyes.

This impossible goal you just wrote down isn't just a thought exercise —it's your training ground. First, we'll explore how to build resilience. Then we'll see how your mind reshapes itself through the pursuit. And finally, we'll learn to reframe how you see the goal altogether.

Why does it feel out of reach? Because most of us live caged by invisible bars—beliefs we've swallowed whole: *I'm not built for this. I've failed before. Others have it easier.* We hit walls and call them fate. But here's the secret the world's greatest minds and toughest souls know: those walls aren't stone. They're smoke. And with the right tools, you can walk straight through them.

This book is your torch. It's going to light up the lies you've believed, burn away the scripts that sabotage you, and show you how to forge a mind that doesn't just survive—it thrives.

The transformative power of this mental approach appears in champions across every field. Take Olympic medalist Alex Ferreira. In 2018, after a devastating crash that doctors said would end his career, he didn't just recover—he dominated. When I asked him how, he didn't talk about physical therapy or training programs. "I decided winning was inevitable," he told me. "I visualized the gold around my neck every night until my brain couldn't imagine any other outcome."

That's not motivation. That's mental warfare. And I'm about to teach you how to fight that battle and win.

What's Waiting Inside

This isn't passive reading. It's a call to action—a blueprint to rewire your brain, reshape your reality, and reclaim your potential. Here's what you'll uncover:

Part I: The Mind—The Foundation of Everything:

Discover how resilience forms the bedrock of mental strength, how challenges literally rewire your brain's capabilities, and why mindset is the only variable you can always control—regardless of circumstances. You need this now because every second you spend with an untrained mind is a second spent living at a fraction of your potential.

Part II: Training Your Mind for Success:

Move beyond motivation to mental systems that deliver results automatically. Master visualization techniques used by Olympic athletes, develop unshakable focus, and learn why gratitude is the secret weapon of elite performers. This isn't "nice to know" information—it's the critical difference between perpetual struggle and breakthrough performance.

Part III: Adapting, Growing, and Thriving:

Transform uncertainty from enemy to ally. Build neural pathways that make adaptation your default setting and install habits that automate success, freeing your conscious mind for higher-level challenges. In a world changing faster than ever, these aren't optional skills—they're survival tools.

Part IV: Shaping Your Life Through Mindset:

Strategically design your environment and relationships to reinforce your mental edge. Create feedback loops that accelerate growth and establish systems for lifelong expansion of your capabilities. Your environment is either sabotaging or supercharging your mental strength every single day—it's time to take control.

Every page is a step closer to that impossible goal you just wrote down. Every chapter is a chance to believe in yourself—not as a hope, but as a fact.

The Bannister Breakthrough

In 1954, Roger Bannister ran a mile in under four minutes—a milestone many believed would literally kill a man. Doctors warned the body couldn't handle the speed. Hearts would rupture. Lungs would give out, they said. Yet he did it, clocking 3:59.4 on a windy

Oxford track. Within a year, dozens followed. Why? Because Bannister didn't just break a record—he broke a belief. Once people saw it was possible, the impossible dissolved.

That's exactly what you're about to experience with your own "four-minute mile." Whatever barrier stands between you and your impossible goal—fear of failure, lack of confidence, uncertainty about your capabilities—it's about to be shattered just as decisively as Bannister's record. The mental tools in these pages will do for your mindset what Bannister did for runners worldwide: prove that the limitations you've accepted as truth are merely temporary beliefs waiting to be broken.

Your First Move

That impossible goal you just wrote down? It's not a someday fantasy. It's not a maybe. Starting right now, it's a deadline. An appointment with destiny that you're going to keep. As we build your *Mental Mastery Pyramid* layer by layer, you'll apply each new tool directly to this goal, systematically dismantling every mental barrier standing in your way.

Turn the page. I'm waiting on the other side with the exact blueprint that's going to rewire your mind for unstoppable achievement. This isn't just about success—it's about becoming the version of yourself that haunts your dreams. Stronger. Unleashed. Inevitable.

The battle above the shoulders begins now.

PART I

THE MIND—THE FOUNDATION OF EVERYTHING

CHAPTER 1: RESILIENCE— YOUR INNER SUPERPOWER

What if the most powerful force in your life isn't your circumstances, your genetics, or even your opportunities—but rather, your ability to push through when every part of you wants to quit? This is about resilience—not just as a concept, but as a super-power you already possess and can strengthen deliberately. It's the quality that separates those who merely dream from those who achieve, and it lives entirely above your shoulders.

The Mental Edge: When Your Mind Decides the Outcome

The referee's whistle sliced the air, but I barely heard it over the pounding in my chest.

Thirty seconds left. Down by one. Trapped.

My body was wrecked—lungs on fire, arms heavy as concrete. I'd fought like hell, but my muscles begged for mercy, whispering an easy excuse: *You've done enough. No one would even know if you stayed down.*

Then, like a bolt of lightning, a single thought cut through the exhaustion:

What if he's just as tired as I am?

The scoreboard said he had the advantage. But did he really? If I was breaking, maybe he was, too. Maybe he was barely holding on, desperate for it to be over.

And that's when everything changed.

I squared my shoulders. Slowed my breath. Faked unbreakable steel.

I wasn't about to let him see my exhaustion. No hesitation, no second-guessing—I exploded with everything I had left. The second I felt his grip weaken, I knew: he cracked first. My brain flipped from prey to predator, adrenaline surging where his fizzled. One shift, one surge, and I reversed him just before the final whistle.

The win was mine.

But the real victory wasn't on the scoreboard. It was up here. Above the shoulders.

I didn't win because I was stronger. I won because I refused to break first. Because I convinced myself I had more left in me, and in doing so, I convinced him he had nothing left. That thought drowned out everything else—the fear, the fatigue, the doubt—leaving only a laser-focused fire in its place.

And that's the lesson that stayed with me:

The mind decides long before the body does.

We all have moments where we think we've hit our limit. But what if we're wrong? What if the only difference between winning and losing is the story we tell ourselves in that moment?

That's what resilience is—not just enduring, but deciding. Deciding that exhaustion, fear, or doubt don't get to make the call. You do.

And once you learn how to tap into that superpower, you start winning battles you never thought you could.

That wrestling match wasn't just a victory—it was my first encounter with what I now call the Mental Determination Framework. In that moment, I unconsciously applied the first principle of this framework: perception shapes performance. When I reframed my opponent as potentially more exhausted than I was, I altered both our realities.

Throughout these pages, we'll build this framework step by step, adding layers of understanding and practical application. What began intuitively on that wrestling mat has evolved into a systematic approach to mental mastery that I've refined through years of testing and application.

What Is Resilience? The Truth I Discovered the Hard Way

I used to think resilience was just about pushing through—until a three-day hike in the Utah wilderness forced me to redefine it entirely.

A friend and I set out to summit the tallest peak, but things quickly went wrong. Heavy snowfall buried the trail, forcing us to set up camp miles short of our goal. The next day, we pushed on, but we fell behind. By the time we reached the summit, we were out of food, out of daylight, and miles from our camp.

That's when I felt it—that cold creep of panic. My heart pounded in my ears. My thoughts scattered like leaves in wind. Every scenario my mind conjured ended badly.

Then I remembered something I had heard a while back: the body obeys the mind.

Panic wasn't going to get us off this mountain—focus would.

I took three deep breaths, steadying my racing thoughts. Then, through the trees, I saw it—a distant campfire flickering in the dark. We pushed through the dense brush, reaching the fire just as the cold set in. The campers let us stay by the fire, giving us a warm place to rest, but without sleeping bags, the night was restless—one side of our bodies warmed by the flames, the other chilled by the open air. At the first light of dawn, we quietly picked ourselves up and found our way back to the trail, ready to finish the journey.

That night changed how I understand resilience. It's not just about physical toughness or "pushing through." It's about controlling your mind precisely when everything around you feels uncontrollable. It's about making the decision to think clearly when your instincts are screaming for you to panic.

Here's the critical distinction I learned on that mountain: Resilience isn't just bouncing back after you've been knocked down. That's recovery—and it's passive. Real resilience is active. It's making the decision to face challenges head-on, adapt when necessary, and push forward precisely when every cell in your body is screaming at you to quit.

Think about that difference for a second. Are you just trying to get back to where you were? Or are you using challenges to become stronger than you were before?

When I was in high school, I was cut from every team I tried out for —first day, every time. I told myself I'd never measure up. Even now, after achieving things I once thought impossible, self-doubt remains my constant companion. At work, I sometimes feel like an impostor, my voice quieter than it should be.

But here's what I've learned: resilience isn't about eliminating doubt —it's about moving forward despite it. You don't need to feel confident to act confident. You don't need to feel strong to be strong. Fear will always be there—the question is whether you let it decide your next move.

While that wrestling match gave me my first taste of mental resilience, it would take experiences like that Utah wilderness night to develop this quality into a consistent force. The growth of resilience isn't a single event but a journey—one that continues to unfold through every challenge we face. And it starts with the battles no one else sees.

The First Battle of the Day: Small Choices, Big Impact

Let me ask you something: What's the first battle you face every single day?

For most of us, it's that moment when the alarm detonates in the early mornings, shattering the silence. Your bed turns traitor, a warm cocoon of false promises. The snooze button sits there, smug, whispering, *Come on. Just five more minutes.*

Your mind joins the mutiny: *No one will know. It's too early. Too cold. Too much.*

Sound familiar?

This is the first fight of the day—the one no one sees, but the one that sets the tone for everything else. The difference between those who rise and those who roll over is not talent, not luck, not even motivation. It's resilience.

Resilience isn't flashy. It doesn't announce itself with grand gestures. It's built in the dark, in the quiet moments when no one is watching. It's forged when you swing your legs out of bed, when you lace up your shoes, when you step into the cold and decide—*I go anyway.*

One morning, after years of fighting the 5 a.m. wake-up battle, something finally shifted. I felt that fierce tug, like Velcro ripping, legs jelly, house silent—but this time, I wasn't my bed's puppet anymore.

"Get up."

The thought was so loud in my head, I half-expected my wife to stir beside me. My body resisted, but my mind had already made the call. No negotiating. No bargaining. Just action.

"Today's mine."

That moment—when hesitation meets determination—is the birthplace of resilience. Like the small act of waking up when you'd rather sleep, resilience is built through these micro-moments of discipline that shape who we become.

My dad once told me that the mind, not the body, is the ultimate battleground. Flip that switch up here, and the game changes. Dad called it 80%—I'd learn he undershot it. I know, because I've lived it.

Each morning victory grooved my brain tougher, stacking proof that I could do hard things when most wouldn't. This wasn't about proving anything to others—it was about proving to myself that I could trust my own word. That when I said I would do something difficult, I would follow through, even when no one was watching.

Are you winning your first battle of the day? Or are you negotiating with yourself before your feet even hit the floor? The way you handle this seemingly insignificant moment reveals more about your mental strength than you might think.

Perhaps nowhere was the power of resilience more evident than in a scorching desert halfway around the world.

The Dune That Broke Me—and Built Me Back Stronger

Look, for most of my life, I thought I knew my limits. That certainty felt safe. Logical, right? Until a scorching desert in Abu Dhabi shattered everything I thought I knew about human endurance.

The Spartan World Championship Beast course was notorious—13 miles through the Empty Quarter, one of the harshest deserts on

Earth. I brought my son to teach him about perseverance. Never thought I'd be the one fighting to survive.

I made a rookie mistake—one energy bar each, no water. I figured the aid stations would be enough.

They weren't. Not even close.

At the barbed wire crawl, my hamstrings locked up so violently I collapsed face-first into the sand. No warning. Just complete shutdown.

Pain like an electrical surge shot through my legs. The sun? Merciless. It hammered down, turning my sweat into salt crystals that scraped my skin raw. And breathing? Each breath pulled more desert into my lungs—so dry it felt like my throat was on fire.

Standing over me, eyes wide with concern, was my son.

"Dad, you good?" His voice was steady, but I could hear the hesitation. He'd been looking to me for strength. And now, he was watching me fall apart.

I nodded. Straight-up lied.

Somewhere ahead, a Spartan photographer had positioned himself at the perfect vantage point—this was one of those moments designed to break racers. A place where quitting wasn't just an option, it was practically expected.

I forced myself up, legs trembling, my entire body screaming at me to stop. This wasn't about finishing anymore. Wasn't even about me. It was about what he would take from this moment.

Then came the Hill of Horrors.

Almost a thousand feet of elevation gain. 50-degree incline. Sand swallowing half of every step.

My mouth was dust. Heat waves danced across the dunes. My feet? Raw meat. My body was breaking down, and my mind was next.

That's when the mind games started.

This is stupid.

No one will care if you stop.

You've done enough. Just sit down.

I collapsed, forearms in the sand, head down. Done.

The Spartan photographer—positioned precisely for moments like these—snapped a picture. A man at his absolute lowest, drained, defeated, questioning whether he could go on.

That photo now hangs in my office. Not as a reminder of weakness, but of choice.

Because in that moment, I wasn't the guy who had run an Ironman. I was just a guy sitting in the sand, on the edge of quitting.

But then I looked up.

My son was still ahead, struggling—but moving.

We locked eyes.

No words. Just a nod.

A silent contract: *We finish.*

I forced myself back to my feet. Head roared stop; I willed three steps forward. Not thirteen miles, not even the whole hill. Just three steps. Then three more.

One step. Another.

Each felt impossible, but here's the thing—impossible is a lie the mind tells the body.

Instead of seeing the entire dune—this mountain of impossibility—I focused on three steps. Then three more. By shrinking my goal to something ridiculously achievable, I bypassed the overwhelm center of my brain and activated the part that could still function.

This approach—what I now call Bite-Sized Wins—became my lifeline not just in that moment, but countless times since. It's the first tool in the Mental Mastery System you're about to build—one piece at a time, each one forged for moments exactly like this.

The sand shifted beneath me, stealing progress. Around me, racers sat down, defeated.

I kept moving.

Did I cross the finish line in a glorious sprint? Hell no. I stumbled through, drained, shattered—but standing.

And beside me? My son.

We collapsed past the finish line, clutching water bottles like lifelines. He turned to me, his voice quiet but certain:

"I get it now."

He tapped his temple. His eyes lit, a kid turned warrior in 13 miles.

It's all up here.

And that made every agonizing step worth it.

Because he didn't just learn about perseverance that day.

He learned that even the strong fall. Even the prepared break. Even the ones who have done it before can be brought to their knees.

And in those moments, the only thing that matters is whether you get back up.

Reframing Setbacks: From Recovery to Rebuilding

While my desert experience taught me about resilience through immediate physical suffering, sometimes the greatest tests of mental fortitude stretch across years. This is where my friend Ashley Caldwell's journey hits different.

Ashley was crushing it as an Olympic aerial skier when back-to-back ACL tears threatened to end her career before it truly began. Most athletes would've seen this as a career death sentence. But during her second rehab, a physical therapist asked her something that changed everything: "Are you rebuilding or just recovering?"

Think about that distinction for a second. Recovery? That's trying to get back what you lost. Rebuilding? That's creating something stronger than before.

"Every setback is an opportunity to rebuild something better than what existed before," Ashley told me years later. "Now my knees are bionic. Operated on by one of the best surgeons in the world. My leg strength numbers were stronger after rehab than before I was injured." We'll return to Ashley's story later, but here's what matters now: this mindset shift doesn't just apply to sports injuries. Whether you're bouncing back from getting fired, dealing with a relationship falling apart, or facing any major setback—the question remains the same: Are you just trying to get back to where you were, or are you rebuilding something better?

This rebuilding mindset represents the first critical mental reframe in your journey above the shoulders. Throughout this book, we'll encounter a series of such reframes—perspective shifts that fundamentally alter how you approach challenges. In Chapter 3, we'll explore how these reframes become automatic, rewiring your default responses to difficulty. But it begins here, with this fundamental distinction: are you just getting back to normal, or creating something better?

The Ultimate Test: Resilience Under Extreme Pressure

The science behind resilience provides powerful evidence for its trainability, but sometimes we need to see these principles tested in the most extreme environments to truly understand their potential. My twin brother's journey through Special Forces training offers exactly that—a laboratory of human endurance where the "above the shoulders" battle determines success or failure.

He wasn't joining the Army for a career. He was joining for one reason: to earn the Green Beret. He knew what that meant—the grueling pipeline, the crushing weight of rucksacks, the sleepless nights, the relentless assessments designed to break men down.

The only thing that mattered was this: When the moment came, he wouldn't quit.

Three hundred soldiers showed up at Camp Mackall, ready to prove themselves. The first test? Land navigation—12-mile treks through the woods, alone, in the dark, carrying a rucksack heavy enough to grind bones. No GPS. No help. Just a compass, a map, and the will to keep moving.

What makes this story remarkable isn't the physical challenge— impressive as it was. It's the mental framework my brother built before he ever set foot in training.

"The physical suffering was guaranteed," he told me later. "So I accepted it in advance. I made a pact with myself: *Pain is coming, and I welcome it. The only variable is my response.*"

This pre-decision—choosing his response before facing the challenge—became his secret weapon. When others were questioning whether they could continue, he had already answered that question months earlier. The debate was closed.

During the most punishing portions of training, when sleep deprivation and hunger clouded judgment, my brother relied on what he called "mental anchors"—simple phrases he could repeat to center himself: *One more step. One more hour. One more day.*

Some got lost. Some gave up.

Then came the physical beatdowns—ruck marches through endless sandpits, carrying logs, flipping tires, grinding through obstacle courses designed to sap every last ounce of strength. Team exercises followed, where failure meant your entire group suffered.

He once told me about a night that nearly broke him. Three days without sleep, soaked to the bone in freezing rain, his team had just failed an exercise. As punishment, they were ordered to stand in formation, at attention, in the downpour.

"My body was shaking uncontrollably," he said. "My mind started playing tricks on me. I began hallucinating. The guy next to me was crying silently. That's when I knew we were all at our limit."

But in that moment, he returned to his anchor: *This pain is temporary. My response is what matters.*

"I started counting my breaths," he told me. "Just focus on the next breath. Then the next. Nothing else exists."

Sleep was a luxury. Food was fuel, nothing more. Every day, they pushed harder, breaking men down until they were nothing but raw determination or empty shells.

"I thought about quitting every single day," my brother admitted later. "But I made that decision before I started. It didn't matter how much it hurt—I was going through."

By the time it was over, more than half the candidates were gone. Some quit. Some collapsed. Some simply weren't selected. But his name was called. He was moving on.

Then came SERE (Survival, Evasion, Resistance, and Escape), the test that broke many. Soldiers were hunted, captured, thrown into isolation, interrogated, and starved. My brother emerged from that experience changed—tougher, sharper, unbreakable.

The biggest lesson? Resilience isn't about not feeling pain. It's about pushing forward despite it.

My brother didn't make it because he was stronger or faster than the others. He made it because he had already decided that nothing— not exhaustion, not fear, not pain—was going to stop him.

The Special Forces pipeline is designed to strip away everything except for that choice: Do you keep going, or do you quit?

He kept going.

And that's why he earned the Green Beret.

What's remarkable is how these mental strategies translate to everyday challenges. When facing that crucial presentation at work that might determine your promotion, are you focused on the discomfort or on your response to it? When dealing with a difficult team member, are you letting their behavior dictate yours, or are you pre-deciding how you'll respond? When pushing through the final sprint to meet a deadline, do you have your own mental anchors to keep you centered?

These aren't just military tactics—they're resilience strategies anyone can use. The battlefield might be different, but the mental game is exactly the same.

. . .

The Spark That Started It All: A Brief Look at My Ironman Journey

Years before that desert race in Abu Dhabi, a colleague's dismissive "You couldn't do an Ironman" became the unlikely spark for one of my most profound lessons in resilience. Despite having no training—I couldn't even swim properly—I committed to a challenge that seemed objectively impossible: a 2.4-mile swim, 112-mile bike ride, and 26.2-mile marathon run.

That initial day struggling to complete even 25 yards in the pool perfectly illustrated the gap between my ambition and ability. But the mind, not the body, would determine my outcome. The fear that gripped me as I dove back in was real, but so was my determination: "I will not fail."

Resilience manifests in the simple act of showing up when every instinct tells you to quit. You'll hear more about that full journey soon. But the spark began here, with a mental shift that transformed doubt into determination—a lesson that would serve me well years later on those crippling dunes of the Spartan race.

Building Your Resilience: The Strategy of Small Wins

Let's cut through the noise. These dramatic stories of resilience under pressure—desert races, military training, Olympic comebacks—they reveal a universal truth that's easily missed: resilience isn't built in single, epic moments. It's developed through countless small victories that compound over time, like interest in a mental bank account.

The three key strategies we've explored so far:

1. **Pre-decision:** My brother's approach of deciding responses before challenges arise

2. Bite-Sized Wins: Breaking overwhelming obstacles into absurdly small steps

3. Rebuilding vs. Recovering: Ashley's framework for transforming setbacks

These tools work in concert, but here's the catch—they must be practiced deliberately in everyday moments.

Think about that decisive moment when you finally break free from the warm grip of your bed on a cold morning. Or when you choose to have the difficult conversation instead of avoiding it. Or when you push through one more repetition when your muscles are screaming to stop.

These seemingly minor choices? They're actually resilience training in disguise. Each one strengthens the neural pathways associated with perseverance, making it easier to access this quality when you need it most.

I call this the "Resilience Scorecard" approach—a simple way to build this capacity deliberately. But listen, here's what most people miss: if you're not actively using this approach, you're losing ground. Your brain is literally rewiring itself every day based on your choices. Every time you hit snooze, avoid the hard conversation, or skip the workout, you're training your brain for surrender, not resilience.

What follows is the cornerstone implementation tool of the entire *Mental Mastery Pyramid*—the system that will thread through every chapter of this book. While the Resilience Scorecard stands powerful on its own, in subsequent chapters we'll add specialized applications and enhancements to this framework. Master this foundation now, and each additional layer will multiply its effectiveness.

THE RESILIENCE SCORECARD

Each day, build your mental toughness with these four straightforward steps:

1. **PICK YOUR CHALLENGE:** Choose one small, specific task for today that pushes your comfort zone slightly.

2. **REFRAME IT:** See it not just as a task but as building your resilience muscle—make it meaningful beyond the action itself.

3. **DO IT DESPITE RESISTANCE:** Feel the discomfort, acknowledge it, then act anyway. Your brain will fight you—expect and overcome it.

4. **TRACK AND REPEAT:** Record your win visibly, creating a chain you won't want to break. Tomorrow, do it again.

Let me share how this worked for me. No theory—real world application.

Several years ago, I struggled with consistent exercise. I'd start strong, then gradually slide back into inactivity. The problem wasn't knowledge or even motivation—it was resilience in the face of discomfort.

I applied the Resilience Scorecard by identifying a ridiculously small daily challenge: putting on my running shoes. That's it. No requirement to actually run—just lace up. I framed it as building my identity as someone who shows up. When resistance appeared (too tired, too busy), I acknowledged it but executed anyway.

After each successful day, I'd mark an X on my calendar. As those X's accumulated, something shifted—not just in my behavior, but in my self-image. I became someone who keeps promises to myself, even when it's hard.

The fascinating result wasn't just a streak of shoe-lacing—it was that once the shoes were on, running naturally followed. By focusing on the smallest point of resistance and consistently overcoming it, the larger challenge became less daunting.

This same approach works brilliantly in professional settings. I once worked with a marketing executive who struggled with debilitating presentation anxiety. Rather than focusing on mastering entire presentations, we applied the Resilience Scorecard to one small element: the first 30 seconds of the introduction. She practiced this opening relentlessly until it became automatic. When presentation day arrived, nailing those first 30 seconds created momentum that carried her through the rest. Within six months, she went from dreading presentations to volunteering for them.

If you're not convinced yet, consider this: research from the University of Pennsylvania shows that small, consistent practices in resilience-building create measurable changes in how the brain processes stress and adversity. This isn't just motivational talk—it's neurological transformation happening in real time with every small victory.

Over time, these small wins compound, creating an upward spiral of capability that carries you through life's greatest challenges—from desert dunes to professional setbacks to personal struggles. And if you're not deliberately building this capacity, you're almost certainly losing it. There is no neutral ground in the battle for mental resilience.

Your Mental Mastery Roadmap

In this chapter, you've acquired the foundational elements of mental resilience—the base of the *Mental Mastery Pyramid* we're building together. You now have:

1. **Strategy: Bite-Sized Wins** - Breaking overwhelming challenges into manageable steps

2. **Mental Reframe: Rebuilding vs. Recovering** - Transforming setbacks into opportunities

3. **Implementation Tool: The Resilience Scorecard** - Your daily practice for building mental toughness

Next, we'll explore how pressure can actually forge new strengths through pressure and challenge—transforming your resilient mind into a powerful forge for creating new capabilities. Each chapter builds upon these core concepts, creating a comprehensive system for mental mastery that's greater than the sum of its parts.

Your Dune Is Waiting

Take a moment now to revisit what you wrote down. Be specific. Name the most challenging aspect of your goal. Break it down into those *Bite-Sized Wins* we talked about. What are the three ridiculously small steps that will start your momentum? Then take that first small action—however insignificant it might seem. That single decision might be the beginning of your own transformation story.

Think about it—recall a time when you overcame something you once thought impossible. That victory wasn't luck or talent or circumstance. That was resilience in action. You have that power within you right now—stronger than your doubts, more enduring than your discomfort, and ready to carry you toward that impossible goal you've set, one resilient choice at a time.

Just like that wrestling match where I found one more push when everything in me wanted to quit—when I asked myself "What if he's just as tired as I am?" and that single thought changed everything—your defining moments will come when exhaustion, doubt, and fear tell you to surrender. But now you know the secret: the mind is the ultimate decider.

But what happens when your mind itself becomes the battlefield? How do we push beyond mere resilience to actually reshape what our minds are capable of?

That's where we turn next—to the forge itself—where through deliberate heat and pressure, your mind becomes not just resilient, but utterly transformed.

The question isn't whether you have what it takes. You do. The question is whether you're ready to step into the forge and emerge as someone new.

CHAPTER 2: THE FORGE OF THE MIND

The workshop was dimly lit, the air thick with the smell of burning oil and scorched metal. Scraps of discarded filaments littered the wooden floors. For months, Thomas Edison and his team had worked tirelessly, testing materials, refining techniques, chasing the impossible dream of electric light.

And for months, they had failed.

One experiment after another ended in disappointment. Glass shattered. Wires melted. Paper-thin filaments burned out in seconds. His team, exhausted and frustrated, began to wonder if they were chasing a fantasy.

But Edison saw it differently.

Each failure, in his eyes, was not an ending but a revelation—one more way that wouldn't work, one step closer to the right answer. "I have not failed," he said, brushing soot from his hands. "I've just found 10,000 ways that won't work."

Then came the moment. A filament—delicate, precise—was placed in the bulb. The current flowed. A glow flickered, held for a second, then two... and stayed. The workshop erupted in celebration. After years of relentless effort, the light had finally been born.

What if Edison had quit at attempt 5,000? Or 9,000? The world as we know it might still be in darkness.

But more importantly, what if setbacks aren't obstacles but the very forge where resilience is shaped? While those desert dunes revealed the foundation of resilience—your ability to endure and persist— now we're digging deeper to understand the neurological machinery that powers that transformation. Edison's story isn't just about persistence—it's the next level of our *Mental Mastery Pyramid*: how the forge of challenge physically reshapes our cognitive architecture.

The Knowledge: Where Ordinary Minds Become Extraordinary

This mental forge—where challenges reshape our capabilities—is perhaps nowhere better illustrated than in the grueling test faced by London's black cab drivers.

Every year, hopeful Londoners take on "The Knowledge"—widely considered one of the hardest tests in the world. To earn the right to drive one of the black cabs, they must memorize 25,000 streets, 320 routes, and thousands of landmarks, all within a six-mile radius of Charing Cross.

For an average of 3 to 4 years, they study by riding scooters through the chaotic city, dodging double-decker buses in the rain, rehearsing routes aloud as if their lives depend on it—because in some ways, their futures do. No GPS, no shortcuts, just pure mental endurance.

To fully appreciate what these aspiring cabbies endure—and what it reveals about your own potential for mental resilience—consider this scenario:

Imagine you've just lost your job. After weeks of rejection letters, you make a decision that surprises even you: you're going to become a London black cab driver. You'll take on The Knowledge.

On your first day, the examiner hands you a Blue Book—six hundred pages of routes to memorize—and simply says, "Start with Manor House Station to Gardnor House." You nod, as if this makes perfect sense, as if you haven't just signed up for what will become the most mentally demanding experience of your life.

That afternoon, you're on a secondhand scooter, crawling through traffic, with rain soaking through your jacket as you attempt to find the most direct route. You do this for twelve hours. Then you do it again the next day. And the next. Weekends. Holidays. In sweltering heat and freezing rain.

For months, you rise at 4 a.m., study routes over coffee, then mount your scooter to physically trace the paths, speaking them aloud to embed them in memory: "Forward Manor House Station, right Seven Sisters Road, comply Green Lanes..." You return home exhausted, only to study maps late into the night.

After eighteen months, you're called for your first appearance—a verbal examination where you stand before an examiner who asks you to recite the perfect route between two random points. The pressure is crushing; your mind goes blank. You fail. Three weeks later, you try again. Fail again.

Many of your fellow candidates have already quit. Some moved back home with parents, others returned to their old jobs. Of the twenty-five who started with you, only eight remain. You work nights as a bartender to pay rent, studying routes during slow shifts. Your social life disappears. Relationships dissolve. But something in you refuses to quit—a conviction that grows stronger with each pre-dawn alarm.

On your fourth appearance, the examiner asks, "Take me from Marble Arch to the Tower of London." Your heart races, but you close your eyes for a moment, visualizing the city from above. Then you begin, "Forward Marble Arch, comply Oxford Street, comply New

Oxford Street..." You describe every turn, every landmark, every one-way system that would affect the journey. When you finish, the examiner merely nods and makes a note.

Three years and fourteen appearances after you began, you receive your green badge—the mark of a licensed London taxi driver. You're now among the elite navigators who can recall the fastest route between any two points in London within seconds, without technology, regardless of traffic conditions or road closures.

What makes this journey remarkable isn't just the feat of memory—it's what happens to the brain in the process.

The Adaptable Mind: How Challenges Reshape Your Brain

Here's the truly extraordinary part: Neuroscientists at University College London have documented how this training physically transforms the brain, providing some of the most compelling evidence of neuroplasticity in healthy adults.

Studies led by Dr. Eleanor Maguire show that London taxi drivers who complete The Knowledge experience significant growth in their posterior hippocampus, the region of the brain responsible for spatial memory and navigation. This means their years of mental effort actually expand their brain's capacity—a rare and compelling example of neuroplasticity in action.

Their minds aren't just learning—they're physically evolving in response to the mental demands placed upon them.

Even more telling, longitudinal studies show these changes develop progressively during the training process and aren't present in candidates who drop out or fail to complete The Knowledge. The brain's adaptation is directly tied to the persistence through difficulty—not innate talent or genetic predisposition.

When I refused to break on that wrestling mat, or took those three more steps in the desert race, my brain wasn't just powering through —it was physically rebuilding itself, creating new neural pathways that would make future challenges easier. The same transformation happening in London cabbies' hippocampi was occurring in my own brain's resilience centers.

This isn't just about cab drivers. It's about what's possible for all of us. If navigating London's maze-like streets can rewire the brain, imagine what happens when you train yourself for mental resilience, focus, and adaptability in the face of your own challenges.

Your brain isn't a fixed machine; it's a dynamic organ that grows stronger through appropriate challenge. Just as physical stress builds muscle when followed by recovery, mental challenges build cognitive resilience when approached with the right mindset.

The Creative Forge: When Mental Limits Meet Persistence

I experienced my own version of this mental forge early in my career, when I was hired as a producer/editor for a high-stakes product video. My first major assignment should have been exciting, but instead it triggered an overwhelming sense of doubt. The blank time-line on my screen might as well have been a vast desert—I felt completely out of my element.

The project required a high-energy style that I could envision but didn't know how to execute. I had a clear mental image of the finished product—dynamic transitions, sophisticated motion graph-ics, a particular visual rhythm that would showcase the product perfectly. But the gap between my vision and my technical abilities seemed impossible to bridge.

Each attempt fell short. The motion graphics wouldn't behave as I needed them to. The energy felt forced. The transitions looked amateur. My internal dialogue became increasingly harsh: *Who am I kidding? I'm not qualified for this.* I was experiencing exactly what London's cabbie trainees feel when they fail their first appearance—the crushing weight of a challenge that exceeds current capabilities.

But something kept me at my desk late into the nights. I wasn't just trying the same approach repeatedly; I was breaking down the problem into smaller components, tackling one specific technical challenge at a time. How do I create this particular animation? What causes this timing issue? Which effect would create the energy I'm visualizing?

What I didn't realize then was that as I moved through each phase—filming certain aspects, building motion graphics, laying down the narration—I was constructing more than just a video. Each step became a building block of confidence. Completing one element successfully gave me the courage to attempt something slightly more complex, creating a scaffolding of small wins that gradually transformed my approach to the entire project.

For days, I cycled between frustration and small breakthroughs. Each tiny victory—figuring out a particular effect, solving a technical limitation—provided just enough momentum to tackle the next obstacle.

On day three, something clicked—literally. I felt it like a physical sensation, a sudden clarity where before there had been only fog. The effect that had seemed impossible 48 hours earlier now appeared obvious, my fingers moving across the keyboard with an assurance I couldn't have imagined when I started. I wasn't conscious of it then, but my brain was physically rewiring itself through this process, forming new neural pathways specific to these challenges.

When I finally rendered the completed video—ahead of deadline and exceeding my own expectations—I experienced a moment of cognitive dissonance. Looking back at my panicked state from just weeks earlier, I couldn't reconcile it with the person who had created this work I was genuinely proud of.

This transformation wasn't just about acquiring technical skills. It was about my brain adapting to a new level of problem-solving, creativity under pressure, and persistence through uncertainty. Like Edison finding thousands of ways that wouldn't work, or the London cabbie failing multiple appearances before mastery, the struggle itself had been the catalyst for growth.

This pattern repeats across every domain of human achievement. Authors face rejection slips, entrepreneurs watch funding evaporate, scientists see experiments fail—and those who persist through these moments often discover that the resistance itself shaped their ultimate success. J.K. Rowling was rejected by twelve publishers. James Dyson created 5,126 failed prototypes before his vacuum design worked. Their minds, like Edison's, like the London cabbies', grew stronger through deliberate confrontation with difficulty.

Small Choices, Lasting Changes: The Power of Micro-Wins

Edison's thousands of "successful failures" that eventually led to the light bulb illustrate something profound about mental resilience: it's rarely built through single dramatic moments but through countless small choices. Each unsuccessful experiment provided Edison with data that ultimately led to breakthrough—a perfect illustration of how micro-wins compound over time.

These micro-choices build your mental muscle now, and later we'll see how they evolve into something automatic through the 1% Solution. They represent the neurological mechanism behind that resilience foundation we've been building.

James Clear articulates this concept perfectly in his work on habit formation: "Every action you take is a vote for the type of person you wish to become." These votes, accumulated over time, represent more than just willpower—they become your identity, reinforcing your capacity to overcome mental resistance with each new challenge.

But unlike physical resilience, which is easier to see, the mental forge operates in subtle, often invisible ways:

Choosing to read a challenging book instead of scrolling social media

Tackling the difficult project before the easy one

Forcing yourself to solve a problem rather than asking for an immediate answer

Writing for thirty minutes when inspiration is nowhere to be found

Learning one new skill that stretches your capabilities

These choices might seem small in isolation. But neuroscience confirms that each one—like the London cabbie studying one more route, or Edison testing one more filament—creates and strengthens neural pathways. The brain physically changes in response to these micro-decisions, becoming more efficient at handling similar challenges in the future.

The Universal Principles of Mental Forging

The brain doesn't fundamentally distinguish between types of challenges—whether you're memorizing London streets, designing light bulbs, or pushing through a desert race. The core neurological processes that build resilience follow similar patterns. These four principles explain precisely why life is 90% above the shoulders— they're the neurological machinery that converts mental choice into physical capability, transforming the impossible into the inevitable:

1. Stress + Recovery = Growth

Just as muscles grow stronger through the cycle of stress and recovery, neural pathways strengthen when challenged and then given time to consolidate. This explains why both London cabbies and elite athletes benefit from spaced, progressive training rather than cramming. Those early challenges made you stronger for a reason—your brain was physically adapting during the recovery periods.

2. Deliberate Difficulty

Not all challenges forge resilience equally. Both Edison and the cabbies engaged in what psychologists call "deliberate practice"—focused effort at the edge of current abilities. Random hardship doesn't build the same neural architecture as purposeful challenge. This is why the "three more steps" approach from the desert race works so effectively—it creates the perfect level of challenge for your brain to adapt to.

3. Persistent Adaptation

The brain's response to challenge isn't uniform but progressive. The hippocampus of London cabbies didn't enlarge overnight; it adapted gradually as the mental demands increased. This principle applies to all forms of mental resilience—consistent effort compounds over time. The wrestling match and desert race stories from Chapter 1 weren't isolated incidents but points on a continuum of progressive neural adaptation.

4. Identity Reinforcement

With each challenge overcome, your brain doesn't just record a success; it updates your identity. The cabbies don't just know London; they become navigators. Edison didn't just invent; he became an innovator. And with each micro-win, you become more resilient. This explains why refusing to break on that wrestling mat wasn't just about winning a match—it was about fundamentally changing how I saw myself.

Building Your Mental Forge: Practical Applications

How do you apply these principles to deliberately strengthen your mental resilience? Consider the following framework for building your own mental forge:

1. Progressive Overload for the Mind

Just as physical trainers prescribe progressively heavier weights to build strength, you can deliberately increase cognitive load to build mental resilience:

If you currently read ten pages daily, try twelve tomorrow, then fifteen next week

If you can focus for twenty minutes, push for twenty-two, then twenty-five

If you speak one language, learn phrases in a second, then simple conversations

The key is gradual progression—challenging enough to stimulate growth but not so overwhelming that it leads to abandonment.

2. The Resilience Scorecard for Mental Challenges

In Chapter 1, we discussed tracking physical resilience. Apply the same principle to mental challenges:

Document daily instances when you chose difficult thinking over easy distraction

Record how you pushed through creative blocks or mental fatigue

Note times when you persisted in learning despite confusion or frustration

This scorecard creates tangible evidence of your growing mental resilience and provides motivation during future challenges.

3. Deliberate Recovery

The London cabbies didn't study 24 hours a day; Edison occasionally slept. The brain, like muscles, requires recovery to solidify gains:

Schedule dedicated downtime after intense mental effort

Use sleep strategically to consolidate learning and creative insights

Implement mindfulness practices to clear mental space between challenges

Recovery isn't weakness—it's the essential partner to challenge in the forging process.

4. Create Your Knowledge

The London Knowledge test provides a template for deliberate mental challenge: comprehensive mastery of a complex domain through persistent effort. What could be your "Knowledge"?

Master a musical instrument from beginner to performance level

Learn a programming language well enough to build a functioning application

Study a complex topic outside your field until you can teach it
to others

The specific domain matters less than the process of sustained
mental effort through progressive difficulty.

The Choice That Forges Greatness

Every day presents countless opportunities to strengthen or weaken
your mental resilience. The brain you have tomorrow will be shaped
by the choices you make today—literally, physically changed by what
you demand of it.

When faced with mental resistance—the urge to quit, to take the easy
path, to avoid the discomfort of deep thought or creative struggle—
picture Edison in his workshop, the London cabbie on their scooter
in the rain, and ask yourself: "Which choice forges the mind I want to
have?"

Because that's the ultimate power of the mental forge—it doesn't just
help you accomplish today's goals; it builds the very instrument with
which you'll tackle every future challenge. Your brain, continuously
shaped by your choices, becomes either a powerful ally or a limiting
constraint.

The research is clear: your mind adapts when you demand it. The
forge awaits—what will you make of it today?

Your Mental Forge Action Step: This week, identify one skill related
to your impossible goal from the Introduction. Choose something
that makes you uncomfortable—that sits just beyond your current
abilities. Commit to fifteen minutes daily practice, documenting each
small breakthrough. Remember: each minute spent at the edge of
your capabilities isn't just building a skill—it's physically recon-
structing your brain into the organ capable of achieving what once
seemed impossible.

Now that we understand how challenges physically forge the mind's capabilities, we're ready to take direct control of this process. Next, you'll learn how to deliberately program your mindset—the control center that shapes which challenges you take on and how you respond. If the forge builds your mental strength, your mindset is the blacksmith who decides what to create.

CHAPTER 3: MINDSET—THE ONLY THING YOU CAN CONTROL

The alarm breaks the silence of early morning. The house is dark, the neighborhood still. The bed holds me like a hostage, warm sheets like gravity pulling me back into unconsciousness. This is where success or failure is determined—not at the finish line, not at the promotion meeting, not at the scale—but right here, in this moment of choice.

This is mindset. Your brain's forge in action.

While the London cabbies built their mental strength navigating city streets, and Edison created the light bulb through thousands of "successful failures," you have your own mental forge each morning when that alarm sounds. Every time you choose to rise despite resistance, you're hammering your resilience into shape, creating the same neural pathways your brain builds during consistent mental effort.

My thoughts wage war: *Five more minutes. You deserve rest. You were up late. No one will know.* These aren't random musings—they're sophisticated saboteurs, disguised as logical reasoning, protecting me from discomfort. They sound so reasonable, so caring. And they're lying to my face.

I've learned a truth that transformed everything: Your brain eaves-drops the second your eyes open. Mutter, "Today's gonna suck," and it hunts for proof—spilled coffee, cranky emails, traffic jerks. But declare, "I'm owning this day," and suddenly you're spotting opportunities, not obstacles. The same day, the same circumstances, but an entirely different experience.

That's mindset: the one thing you always control, your mental cockpit in life's storm. This isn't Instagram fluff. This is your brain's operating system, and neuroscience confirms you can hack it. This chapter is your upgrade kit: part brain science, part wakesurf wipeout, delivered with a kick of "damn, I can do this."

Just like my dad said in the intro—sports are *"80% above the shoulders."* But as I showed you through the wrestling mat, the desert, and the Ironman course, I've learned life is 90% what happens up here—in that battlefield between your ears. Master that space, and everything else follows. Mental resilience isn't just enduring—it's becoming fireproof.

The 5-Second Launch Code: Programming Your Mind Before Your Feet Hit the Floor

Your brain's like a smartphone. The first app you open determines what runs in the background all day. Your brain's eavesdropping, soaking up whatever you feed it.

If your first thought is, *Today is going to be a nightmare*, your brain's spotlight—the Reticular Activating System—starts scanning for evidence to confirm your prediction. But plant your feet and declare, *Today is going to be a great day*, and you're programming it to hunt for wins instead of losses.

Those first five seconds after waking are your brain's most programmable moment—like accessing your mental source code before the usual programs start running. This morning code operates on the same pre-decision principle I learned from my brother's Special Forces training—deciding your response before the challenge arrives. Just as he prepared his mind for extreme stress before experiencing it, your morning declaration programs your response pattern before facing the day's obstacles.

I discovered this through my wakesurfing obsession. Lake Norman, North Carolina. The water glassy at dawn, the air heavy with possibility. My fixation stretched across two full summers—I wasn't out there every day, but I was there enough that my inability to land a 360-degree spin became almost comical.

For months, I'd carve, spin, then eat lake at 11 mph, sinuses burning with that unmistakable sensation of water forced up your nose at speed. My kids cackling from the boat as I resurfaced, pride drowning faster than my body. "Dad wiped out AGAIN!" they'd howl, pointing at the splash zone I'd created. At first they laughed at every spectacular wipeout, but as time passed, they became my biggest supporters, scanning YouTube tutorials with me, offering increasingly serious advice from the boat.

"You're leaning too far back!" my daughter would shout, her hands cupped around her mouth. "Rotate your shoulders more!" my son would add, mimicking the motion with his own small frame.

After yet another day of failures, muscles aching in places I hadn't felt in years, I caught myself muttering, "This is hopeless." The words tasted bitter, like lake water and defeat. But something clicked in that moment. If I'd get tossed around regardless, why not choose a different mental soundtrack?

The next time I went out, before doubt could creep in, I planted my feet on the cool hardwood floor, locked eyes with my reflection, and declared, "I'm unstoppable." The words felt foreign, almost ridiculous coming out of my mouth. Didn't nail the 360 that day. Or the next. But something shifted in how I approached each attempt. Each crash became data—"more weight on the back foot," "rotate shoulders faster," "look through the turn not down at the board." Not failure, but feedback.

When I finally landed it, after nearly two summers of trying, my kids erupted with genuine excitement. There were cheers from the boat, high-fives all around. It wasn't just my victory anymore; we'd all been on this journey.

Science backs this up. Your brain's neuroplasticity responds to repetition. Those morning declarations aren't just positive thinking; they're neural coding, etching resilience into your gray matter.

What's your morning mental code? Tomorrow, before checking your phone or fully opening your eyes, declare "I'm unstoppable today." Say it like you mean it, like your life depends on it. Then watch what happens by noon.

The Mindset Cage Match: Fixed vs. Growth

Your brain's a forest. A fixed mindset plants concrete—nothing grows. A growth mindset? Fertile soil where even the smallest efforts flourish.

Ever tell yourself, "I'm just not good at this" or "I don't have the talent"? That's what Stanford psychologist Carol Dweck calls a fixed mindset—believing your abilities are set in stone, like they came pre-installed at birth.

A fixed mindset is an old flip phone—limited, clunky, resistant to change. "This is who I am. Failure means I'm not enough."

The alternative is a growth mindset—the latest smartphone, constantly evolving. "I'm not there yet, but I can develop this ability. Failure is just feedback."

This isn't just psychology—it's biology. Brain scans show growth folks light up their command center, not their fear zone. When you push through challenges with a growth perspective, neuroplasticity kicks in, laying down new neural pathways. You literally upgrade your mental hardware.

When I collapsed on that desert dune, I was at a mindset crossroads —fixed mindset said "you're done," while growth mindset asked "what's one more step?" That same choice presented itself to Edison after thousands of failed attempts and to the London cabbies after failed appearances. The distinction isn't just theoretical—it's the fundamental choice that determines whether challenges strengthen or defeat you.

That wakesurfing challenge I mentioned earlier? It's the perfect example of these mindsets in action. After countless wipeouts trying to land that 360 spin, the fixed mindset voice started its campaign: "Maybe you're too old for this. Some people just can't do it."

But the breakthrough came when I shifted from "I can't do this" to "I haven't figured it out YET."

That three-letter word—YET—might be the most powerful in the English language. It transforms every period into a comma, every ending into a checkpoint, every failure into a step forward.

When I finally landed the 360, nothing had changed physically. My muscles hadn't transformed overnight. The only difference was what happened above the shoulders. My mind finally forged the connections my body followed.

That impossible goal you identified in the Introduction? That's your 360 right now. Are you telling yourself you can't achieve it, or you can't achieve it YET? The difference between these two perspectives will determine whether you experience that goal as an insurmountable wall or a challenge you're gradually figuring out how to overcome.

The Housekeepers Who Hacked Their Bodies

Think mindset is just motivation? Think again. Your beliefs literally reshape your physical reality.

One of the most compelling examples of this comes from a remarkable study of hotel housekeepers. These workers hauled, scrubbed, and sweated all day. By any measure, it was a serious workout. But when Harvard researcher Dr. Ellen Langer asked if they exercised regularly, most said no. Despite doing CrossFit-level work for eight hours daily, they didn't see it as exercise—just their job.

Langer split the housekeepers into two groups. She told one group the truth: their work exceeded the Surgeon General's recommendations for an active lifestyle, showing them exactly how many calories each task burned. The control group? They got zero information.

A month later—without changing anything about their work—the informed group showed measurable physical changes. They dropped an average of two pounds. Their blood pressure fell by 10 points. Their body fat decreased.

The control group? Nothing changed.

The first time I heard about this study, I was floored. I remember putting down the article and just sitting there, processing what it meant. If that doesn't scream how powerful our minds are, I don't know what does. Think about it—these people lost weight, lowered their blood pressure, and decreased body fat percentages simply because they were told the truth about the work they were already doing. Their bodies literally transformed because their perception shifted. No diet changes, no extra workouts—just a new understanding of what they were already doing.

Look at your daily grind. What activity do you dismiss as "just a chore"? How might reframing it transform not just how you feel, but what your body actually does with it?

The Superior Mindset: Acting As If Until It's Real

The housekeepers' transformation wasn't just physical—it was proof that our beliefs literally reshape our reality. This same principle extends beyond our bodies to our behaviors, performance, and ultimately, our results.

What separates high achievers? While most people let thoughts spiral into worst-case scenarios, superior performers follow a different algorithm:

1. **Choke negativity fast** - Kill toxic thoughts before they root

2. **Lock on excellence** - Focus on performing at your best, not avoiding failure

3. **Act like you've already won** - Carry yourself as though success is inevitable

You might think, "But I've never done this before—how can I focus on excellence?"

Use your imagination. Literally.

Your brain can't distinguish between a vividly imagined event and reality. When you mentally rehearse success with enough detail, your brain forms the same neural pathways as if you'd physically experienced it.

This works beyond sports. Navy SEALs use it for combat. Surgeons use it before complex procedures. Musicians use it before performances. It's the Mental Movie Method—creating internal simulations so vivid your brain and body respond as though you've already succeeded.

Want to feel confident? Act as if you already are. Your body can't tell the difference between real and simulated confidence, and soon, neither will your mind.

I've seen this principle transform people across countless fields— from athletes visualizing their perfect performance to entrepreneurs embodying the leadership presence they aspire to develop. What makes this approach so powerful is that it's not just psychological trickery; it's neurological rewiring—a direct application of the same mental forging we've already explored.

Think about it this way: your brain processes an expertly visualized scenario using many of the same neural networks it would use during an actual experience. When you vividly imagine yourself speaking confidently, making bold decisions, or performing at your peak, you're literally training your brain to recognize these states as normal and achievable.

The key is specificity and consistency. Vague affirmations won't cut it. You need detailed mental movies—complete with sights, sounds, feelings, and even smells of success. The more senses you engage, the more real it becomes to your brain.

This isn't deception—it's strategic alignment. It's ensuring your behavior matches your ambitions rather than your fears. It's recognizing that sometimes, you need to embody the person you're becoming before external reality catches up.

The Moving Day Challenge: From Chaos to Control

What's the difference between an obstacle and an opportunity? About six inches—the distance between your ears.

When a friend called me in a panic about an upcoming move, I didn't think much of it—until I arrived at the apartment. What greeted me was pure chaos: furniture dismantled into unrecognizable pieces, half-packed boxes spilling their contents, mountains of clothes with no apparent organization. The moving truck was scheduled to arrive in just five hours, and nothing was ready.

"I'm totally screwed," my friend said, voice tight with stress. "I started last night but got overwhelmed. There's no way we can finish this."

My first thought was immediate and visceral: *"What the hell have you been doing all this time? This is a complete disaster."* My stomach tightened, my shoulders tensed..

But then I caught that thought. I recognized it as the exact type of mental sabotage we've been discussing. Standing in that doorway, I made a conscious choice to reframe the situation: "This isn't a disaster—it's a puzzle to solve, one room at a time."

I felt my breathing slow down, my shoulders drop. "We've got this," I said. "Let's break it down into smaller pieces."

That simple mental shift changed everything. Instead of seeing an overwhelming mess, I saw a series of manageable challenges. We created a system—kitchen items first, then bedroom, closets last. Each completed box became a small victory, building momentum for the next task.

"Let's just focus on filling this one box," I told my stressed-out friend, who was verging on giving up. "Then we'll fill another one."

An hour in, my friend's entire demeanor had changed. "This actually feels doable now," he said, sealing up a box of kitchen items. "I was making it bigger in my head than it really was."

Four hours later, we stood surrounded by neatly labeled boxes, disassembled furniture wrapped and ready, with time to spare before the movers arrived. My friend looked at me in disbelief: "How did we pull this off?"

The physical work hadn't changed—we still had to pack the same amount of stuff in the same amount of time. What changed was our perception of the task. By breaking it down and reframing it as a series of achievable steps rather than one overwhelming challenge, we transformed what seemed impossible into something not just doable, but almost enjoyable.

This is the same *Bite-Sized Wins* mindset I used during that desert race—where one monstrous sand dune became manageable when I focused on just three more steps. The moving day challenge responded to the exact same shift: breaking the overwhelming into something winnable through perspective and micro-action.

What "moving day disaster" are you facing right now? A project deadline that seems impossible? A cluttered inbox with hundreds of unanswered messages? A difficult conversation you've been avoiding? Take a moment to identify it, then ask: "How could I reframe this as an interesting puzzle to solve rather than a burden to bear?"

Morning Rituals: Training Your Brain Through Deliberate Discomfort

I dread the cold plunge every morning—body rebels, mind bargains. But I've learned that these moments of resistance—when everything in you screams for the easier route—are exactly where growth happens. They're the practical, daily equivalent of Edison's 10,000 attempts or the London cabbie's years of study—deliberately forging mental strength through challenge.

Every morning, after the sauna, I force myself into freezing water. The mere thought makes me hesitate. My heart rate accelerates before I even touch the water. My breath shortens. My mind starts generating excuses: *Maybe I should skip it today. I didn't sleep well. I'm already running late. I deserve a break.*

Yet I do it anyway, because these dread moments build resilience. Like lifting weights for your mind.

The first touch of cold is always a shock. My skin tightens, goosebumps erupt across my body. The initial plunge sends electricity through every nerve ending. My lungs seize, and for a moment, I can't breathe. Every cell screams to get out.

But I stay. Ten seconds. Twenty. Thirty. The initial shock subsides, replaced by a strange clarity. My breathing steadies. My mind, scattered just moments before, becomes laser-focused on the present. Nothing exists except this moment, this breath, this challenge.

Cold shocks my brain, firing norepinephrine, building synapses. When you step into that plunge, your brain's command center (that's the prefrontal cortex, if you're into the science) flexes its muscle, over-riding the fear center's whining protests. Recent neuroscience research shows that controlled exposure to this kind of stress actually increases neural growth factors like BDNF—essentially fertilizing your brain to grow stronger connections. Brain scans hint at it: more brain connections form in the areas that help you stay calm under pressure—the same mental muscles you need for life's bigger chal-lenges. It's not just a cold dip—it's a workout for grit.

What makes these morning challenges powerful is the identity shift with each repetition. Every time you choose discomfort over comfort, you declare: "I am someone who does hard things." This isn't just something you do—it becomes who you are.

These deliberate discomfort moments aren't just physical challenges —they're training grounds for life's inevitable frustrations. One after-noon, stuck with a frustrating customer service rep—order wrong, hold music still drilling my skull for the fourth time in 30 minutes—I felt oddly calm. No racing heart, no tight chest. I'd have lost it before —now I didn't.

"Sir, I'm sorry, but there's nothing more I can do about your order," the rep said, her voice flat with rehearsed finality.

In the past, this would have triggered an immediate stress response— elevated heart rate, tightened jaw, that rush of heat to my face that signals impending anger. But instead, I noticed a strange familiarity to the sensation. A challenge presented, an urge to escape, and a choice about how to respond.

Then it clicked. I was tapping the same mental pathways I'd strength-ened through those cold plunges. The sensation was familiar—initial resistance, urge to escape, then the disciplined choice to engage anyway. That's the prefrontal cortex holding the reins, honed by mornings of deliberate discomfort.

"I understand this is challenging," I heard myself say calmly. "Let's try a different approach." Fifteen minutes later, we had found a solution that worked for both of us.

These rituals remind me daily: I control my responses, even when I can't control circumstances. I can't stop the water from being cold, but I can decide to face it. Each time I push through, I prove discomfort doesn't own me—I do.

What's your cold plunge equivalent—something brief, uncomfortable, but strengthening—that you could add to your routine? Maybe it's a 60-second silent sit, no phone, just you and your restless brain. Or a quick task you hate—like making the bed—done before coffee. Small wins stack up.

Time to Practice: Take 60 seconds to design your own deliberate discomfort ritual:

1. Identify one small, uncomfortable action for daily practice (e.g., skip the snooze, cold shower).

2. Specify exactly when you'll do it (e.g., right after waking, post-brushing teeth).

3. Write down how this specific discomfort might strengthen your mental resilience (e.g., "Teaches me to act despite dread").

Commit to it for just one week. Even 30 seconds, embraced deliberately, can nudge your neural pathways toward resilience. Start small, level up later—your brain will adapt, and so will you.

Your Mindset Playbook: The Pause & Pivot Technique

Ever notice how pilots handle turbulence? They don't panic—they pause, assess, adjust. Your mind can learn this too.

After studying high performers across various fields, I've found a powerful technique I call *Pause & Pivot*—a simple two-step process you can use anywhere to reset your mindset:

Step 1: Pause and Breathe

When setbacks hit, take three slow, deep breaths. Inhale through your nose for four counts, exhale through your mouth for six. This activates your parasympathetic nervous system, interrupting stress and bringing your prefrontal cortex back online.

This pause creates critical space between stimulus and response. It's in this space—those few seconds between what happens to you and how you react—that your freedom exists.

Step 2: Pivot with a Question

Once you've reset, ask yourself: *"What's one small step I can take right now?"*

This simple shift moves your brain from problem-focused to solution-focused, from victim to empowered.

I used this during a particularly chaotic travel day—delays were stacking up, connections were missed, and stress was mounting all around me. Then the gate agent announced our flight had been canceled due to mechanical issues.

Around me, passengers erupted in frustration. Some demanded immediate solutions, others slumped in defeat. I felt that familiar tightness in my chest, the surge of adrenaline that accompanies disrupted plans.

But instead of diving into that emotional spiral, I caught myself. Breathed in for four counts. Held it. Exhaled for six. Did it three times.

In that brief pause, I felt my nervous system reset, like rebooting a computer. Then I asked myself: "What's one small step I can take right now?" The answer came immediately: "Find out what alternative flights are available."

While others were still processing their reactions, I was already investigating alternative routes and speaking with another airline representative. From there, each small step led to another solution, building momentum instead of despair.

What could have been a day of mounting helplessness became a reminder that while circumstances escape control, my response never does. Those few seconds of pausing and pivoting transformed not just my actions, but my entire experience.

Try This: Instead of a written exercise, take a moment right now to:

1. Think of a recent frustration—something small but annoying that happened in the last week.

2. Close your eyes and take those three deep breaths (4 count in, 6 count out).

3. Feel the slight shift in your body as your shoulders relax.

4. Now imagine asking yourself in that moment: "What's one small step I can take?"

5. Notice how your perspective changes, how solutions begin to appear.

This mental rehearsal primes your brain to use this technique when you need it most, creating new neural pathways that make the *Pause & Pivot* response increasingly automatic.

The 1% Solution: Small Steps to Major Transformation

Improve by just 1% daily, and after a year, you're 37 times better than when you started. This principle transformed my approach to growth.

A few years ago, my family and I faced a decision. We had settled into a comfortable routine in Utah, but we sensed this comfort might be limiting our growth. Our neighborhood was familiar, our friends established, our routines predictable. The kids had their schools, their activities, their social circles. Everything was... great.

When an opportunity arose to relocate to North Carolina, we faced a choice that would ripple through every aspect of our lives. This wasn't forced on us; it was a deliberate decision to step into the unknown, to trade comfort for growth.

"Do we really want to leave everything we know?" my wife asked one night as we sat on the back porch, the Utah mountains silhouetted against the twilight sky.

"It's terrifying," I admitted. "But I keep wondering if we're teaching the kids to choose safety over growth."

The move itself was chaos—a blur of boxes, goodbyes, and long drives. The first month in our new home brought waves of doubt. Had we made a mistake? The kids struggled to adjust, missed their friends, complained about differences in the new school.

But then, almost imperceptibly, things began to shift. I watched my oldest daughter, who had been reserved and hesitant in Utah, thrive in her new job—making friends, becoming someone management relied on for challenging situations. She developed such impressive customer communication skills that she was often the person they'd call in to handle difficult interactions.

"I was scared at first," she told me one evening, "but now I kind of like that feeling of figuring things out from scratch."

All four of my kids thrived in the chaos, developing resilience and confidence they might never have found in our comfort zone. Small, repeated challenges rewired their brains (that's the fancy term "neu-roplasticity" in action), creating good kinds of stress that improved their focus and problem-solving abilities.

This experience illustrated the progressive nature of mental growth. Just like Edison's inventions emerged through relentless iteration and the London cabbies built mental maps one street at a time, my kids' confidence and capability grew by stretching just beyond their comfort zone—day after day.

You might not move cross-country, but you can find small actions that compound toward your impossible goal. Try this "30-Day Challenge": identify one small action daily that nudges you toward that seem-ingly unreachable dream you wrote down in the Introduction. Make each step so tiny it feels almost insignificant—maybe it's researching one aspect of your goal for 10 minutes, making a single phone call, or practicing a relevant skill for just 15 minutes. By day 30, you'll be amazed not just at the cumulative effect, but at how much closer that "impossible" goal suddenly appears.

These micro-challenges aren't just activities—they're identity-building moments transforming who you believe yourself to be.

Grit's Dirty Secret: The Science of Sticking It Out

Picture your brain as a forest. Each time you push through difficulty, you carve a path. The more you travel it, the clearer it becomes until perseverance isn't a choice—it's your default direction.

Want to know why talent's overrated? Angela Duckworth's research shows that stick-with-it-ness trumps natural ability nearly every time.

Each time you push past resistance, your prefrontal cortex activates, releasing dopamine that reinforces your persistence pathway. You're literally rewiring your brain to persist longer each time you refuse to quit.

I experienced this firsthand early in my career. I was working a physically demanding job packing boxes during the day, while spending my evenings learning video editing. My early attempts were rough, and feedback was often discouraging. But I kept showing up, kept improving. Eventually, that consistent effort paid off with my first real editing opportunity. Nothing changed overnight—it was the accumulated effect of hundreds of hours of practice, even when progress seemed invisible.

Most people quit when results lag. They try something new, decide they "lack talent," and move on. They never learn what might have happened if they'd pushed just a little further.

Where could you apply more grit today? What tiny step could move you forward? Remember, persistence isn't sexy, but it's undefeated.

When Mindset Fails: My Darkest Hour

Let me be clear: Developing a superior mindset doesn't mean you'll never face crushing doubt. I've been there—further down than I care to admit.

I was leading a production team for a major event, and the workload was overwhelming. To stay on top of it, I brought in a trusted friend to help with video editing. He was talented, but his workspace was chaotic—hard drives everywhere.

With just weeks to go, disaster struck. He tripped over a cable connected to a working hard drive, sending it crashing to the floor. The files were gone. Unretrievable. Three weeks of footage—interviews, b-roll, crucial segments that couldn't be reshot. My heart nearly dropped out of my chest when he called.

"I'm so sorry," he said, his voice cracking. "I've tried everything. The drive is completely dead."

For a moment, I couldn't speak. A wave of nausea washed over me as I calculated what this meant: missed deadlines, disappointed clients, potentially career-ending failure. My mind raced through worst-case scenarios, each more catastrophic than the last.

The room seemed to spin. I could feel sweat beading on my forehead, my mouth gone dry. This wasn't just a technical problem—it was a moment that could define my career, my reputation, everything I'd worked for. The weight of it was crushing.

But panic wasn't an option. There was no time to dwell on what we'd lost—only time to figure out a way forward.

"Let's think," I said finally, forcing my voice to remain steady. "What do we have? What can we salvage?"

We put our heads together, searched every available system, and found rendered files stored on an internal drive. It wasn't perfect, but it was enough. We rebuilt what we could, and against the odds, we delivered.

The client never knew how close we came to complete failure. The event was a success, but more importantly, I learned something I couldn't have discovered any other way.

That moment taught me something critical: resilience isn't about avoiding setbacks—it's about how you respond when they happen. When the worst-case scenario hits, do you freeze? Or do you focus, adapt, and move forward?

What's your equivalent crisis point right now? It might not be as dramatic as a crashed hard drive with three weeks of irreplaceable work, but identify the situation where your mindset is being tested most severely. Now ask yourself: "What do I still have? What can I salvage?"

The One-Second Rule: When Everything Changes

Let me tell you a personal truth: I wasn't good at team sports in high school. I tried out for soccer, basketball, baseball—and got cut from every team. I still remember scanning the team rosters posted outside the gym, running my finger down the list of names, and feeling that knot in my stomach when mine wasn't there. And to be honest, I hadn't put in the work others had. I hadn't played organized sports growing up, hadn't developed the skills that come from years of practice.

Each rejection stung, but looking back, I recognize they were fair. The kids who made those teams had been playing since they were little. I was jumping in late with no foundation. But even knowing that, it was hard not to take those cuts personally.

By junior year, I was ready to give up on sports entirely. But my twin brother, who had wrestled the previous year, encouraged me to try something different.

"Wrestling's not about what you've done before," he told me one night. "It's about what you're willing to do now. It's about heart, not history."

I remember looking at him skeptically. "Easy for you to say."

"Wrestling doesn't care about any of that," he said. "It only cares if you're willing to suffer more than the other guy. That's something you can choose."

Wrestling was unlike anything I'd tried—grueling practices that demanded mental toughness more than natural talent. The first week, I threw up twice from exertion. My body ached in places I didn't know could ache. Every fiber of my being wanted to quit.

One particularly exhausting practice, I found myself paired with the team captain for drills. He was destroying me, move after move, takedown after takedown. I was exhausted, embarrassed, ready to walk off the mat and never come back.

In that moment, sprawled on the mat, gasping for breath, I faced a choice: get up one more time or stay down. Just one second of decision. Everything in me wanted to stay down, to accept defeat, to walk away with what little dignity I had left.

But I didn't. I got up. Not because I suddenly believed I could win—I knew I couldn't—but because I decided, in that one second, that I wouldn't be the one to break first.

The captain slammed me down again. And again, I got up. Each time, just one second of choice. Each time, just deciding for one moment to continue.

By the end of the season, I wasn't the most technically skilled wrestler on the team. But I had become something more valuable— the guy who simply refused to stay down. Each time I rose from the mat, I wasn't just continuing a match; I was building my "never quit" identity, one painful decision at a time. That reputation followed me, but more importantly, it changed how I saw myself. I was forging the mental DNA that would later carry me through desert races, mountain climbs, and Ironman finish lines.

This is the same fundamental choice I faced during that desert race —that critical moment when my body screamed to stop but something deeper said "three more steps." It's the same shift I experienced on that wrestling mat—the first time I truly understood the power of the mind over the body. These aren't isolated techniques or separate breakthroughs. They're all expressions of one core truth: in your hardest moments, a single second of decision can change everything.

What I learned wasn't just technique—it was the power of persistence. Progress isn't about talent but tenacity, proving success was a matter of "when," not "if."

The One-Second Rule isn't about overnight transformation. It's about making one choice, for one second, even when everything in you wants to quit. Sometimes all it takes is hanging on for that extra moment—one more "I will"—and what seemed impossible suddenly cracks open.

This principle applies far beyond sports. It's about that moment in a difficult conversation when you choose vulnerability instead of defensiveness. It's about pausing before responding to a provocative email. It's about taking one more step toward your goal when all evidence suggests you should quit.

Look, I'm not special. I don't have superhuman willpower or exceptional talents. What I've developed is a mindset that refuses to accept permanent limitations—and you can too.

What's your "one-second choice" right now? Where are you just one decision away from breakthrough? Identify it. Name it. Write it down. Then make the choice your future self will thank you for—not tomorrow, but today.

Remember, success isn't about luck or perfect genes. It becomes inevitable when you master what happens above the shoulders.

Mindset Toolkit at a Glance

We've covered significant ground in this chapter, exploring how your mind shapes reality in ways both subtle and profound. From the housekeepers who transformed their bodies through belief to the cold plunge that builds mental toughness, these concepts all point to one truth: your mindset is the most powerful tool you possess.

These mindset tools don't operate in isolation—they're part of a progressive system. They build on the resilience forged through adversity and the mental strength sharpened under pressure:

5-Second Launch Code: A morning ritual that sets your brain's filter for the day—pre-wiring how you respond before challenges arrive

Deliberate Discomfort: Daily neural strengthening through voluntary challenge. Resistance becomes training

Pause & Pivot: A rapid reset for high-stress moments—creating space between stimulus and response

One-Second Rule: A breakthrough tool for decision points when everything in you wants to quit

1% Solution: A compound growth strategy that transforms small actions into massive gains over time

These aren't just isolated techniques—they're your complete mindset toolkit, working together to help you master what happens above the shoulders. But a toolkit is only valuable when you put it to use, which is why I'd like you to take a moment for some personal reflection.

Mindset Journal: Your Mental Operating System

Choose one of these reflections that resonates most strongly with you:

1. **Morning Launch Code:** What's your typical first thought upon waking? How might changing it affect your day?

2. **Growth Edge:** Identify something you've told yourself you "can't do." Rewrite it with "yet" at the end. How does this shift feel?

3. **Deliberate Discomfort:** What small, uncomfortable action will you take daily this week?

Spend 2-3 minutes exploring this single question deeply rather than rushing through all three. This focused reflection will create a stronger neural imprint than a surface-level consideration of multiple concepts.

This isn't just understanding—it's committing to action. These insights represent your first micro-wins in mindset transformation, the initial steps in rewiring your brain's operating system.

Your Next Battleground

You've now upgraded your mindset operating system with powerful tools that give you control of your mental environment. But even the strongest mindset can be hijacked by the stories you tell yourself—narratives that run so deep you might not even recognize them as optional rather than inevitable.

Next we'll examine how these internal narratives—often running below conscious awareness—shape everything from your daily decisions to your life's trajectory. These identity scripts aren't just passive thoughts—they're sophisticated neural networks, reinforced over decades, that often make your decisions before you even realize it.

The tools you've learned in this chapter—from the 5-Second Launch Code to the One-Second Rule—will become essential allies as we tackle these deeper scripts. The ability to pause, reframe, and choose your response will be critical when confronting the stories that have defined your limits for years.

As we continue our journey above the shoulders, remember this fundamental truth: your mindset is the only battle you're guaranteed to control, and mastering it changes everything else.

CHAPTER 4: THE STORIES WE TELL OURSELVES—ARE YOU SETTING YOURSELF UP TO WIN OR LOSE?

The Seed That Grew into a Weed

For years, I struggled with a narrative that was poisoning my work life. I felt under-appreciated and overlooked, despite pouring myself into marketing plans, photo shoots, and athlete interviews. I was building something I believed was special, yet no one seemed to notice.

What began as a small negative thought—a seed planted in fertile soil—soon grew. At first, I confined these complaints to conversations with my wife and closest friend, seeking their sympathy. Then, almost imperceptibly, the negativity expanded. Small remarks to coworkers. Offhand comments in meetings. Eventually, this seed grew into full-blown conversations where I positioned myself as the victim of an unfair system.

Like any invasive weed, this narrative didn't stay contained. It spread beyond work, affecting my sleep, my relationships, my peace of mind. I would lie awake, replaying scenarios and nursing my resentment, convinced I deserved more recognition than I was receiving. The more I focused on this story, the more exhausted and bitter I became

—physically tense, emotionally drained, mentally trapped in an endless loop of perceived injustice.

Then one sleepless night, an unexpected thought broke through: The very people I resented had given me an extraordinary opportunity. They had hired me for a role I wasn't fully qualified for. They had believed in me when my resume didn't justify it. They had taken a chance on my potential.

The realization hit me like a physical force—a wave of shame followed by clarity. I had been so focused on what I wasn't getting that I had completely overlooked what I had been given. That night, unable to sleep with this new perspective burning in my mind, I reached for my phone in the darkness. Lying there in bed, the soft glow illuminating my face, I crafted an email expressing my genuine gratitude for the opportunity they had provided and apologizing for not acknowledging it sooner. The truth couldn't wait until morning— it needed to be captured while this moment of clarity was still raw and real.

After sending that message, I felt a weight lift from my shoulders— literally. The tension that had been building in my neck and back for months began to release. Colors seemed brighter. Conversations flowed more easily. It was as though that choking weed had been pulled out by its roots, making room for something life-giving to grow in its place—gratitude, perspective, appreciation.

This experience taught me something profound: The stories we tell ourselves don't just reflect our reality—they create it, down to the physical sensations in our bodies and the quality of our daily experiences.

"Your mind isn't just observing your story—it's simultaneously writing, directing, and starring in it."

Resilience helps you endure. Mental forging strengthens your capacity. But the stories you tell yourself determine how those tools get used. Your mindset might be the only thing you truly control—but your personal narrative is what gives that mindset direction and power.

The Script You're Living By

If your life were a movie, what kind of story would it tell? A high-stakes adventure where the hero overcomes impossible odds? A character-driven drama filled with growth and revelation? Or a low-budget production where the main character simply reacts to whatever happens?

The human brain is a storytelling machine. Its primary job isn't to deliver truth—it's to create coherence, to make sense of the world around us. And once we establish a narrative, our minds work tirelessly to reinforce it, often ignoring evidence that contradicts our story while amplifying anything that confirms it.

"I'm not a leader—I don't have that natural confidence." "I've always been bad with money." "Success comes easier for other people." "I'll never be in great shape."

None of these is objective truths. They are simply scripts you've accepted as reality. This explains why two people can experience the same event yet walk away with completely different interpretations. The event didn't change—but the lens through which they viewed it did.

Confirmation Bias: Your Mind's Evidence-Gathering System

Your mind is constantly searching for evidence to confirm your beliefs. If you tell yourself that nothing ever works out, your brain will begin scanning for proof—highlighting every setback, every inconvenience, and every failure. It's not that life is objectively worse;

it's that your brain is simply doing its job, reinforcing the story you've chosen to tell.

But here's the key: This works both ways.

If you start asking yourself, "How can things get better?" or "What good is happening in my life?", your brain will shift its focus. It will begin seeking out small victories, moments of growth, and hidden opportunities—gradually reshaping your perception toward hope and possibility.

Confirmation bias isn't your enemy; it's a tool waiting for better instructions. Tell it what to confirm.

Your Brain's Filtering System

Your brain operates using something called the Reticular Activating System (RAS)—a network of neurons that filters what gets your attention. It's the same mechanism you trained with the 5-Second Launch Code—programming your mental spotlight before the day even begins.

Right now, there are millions of pieces of information around you, but your brain can't process them all. Instead, it locks onto whatever aligns with your dominant thoughts and beliefs.

Ever notice that when you learn a new word, you suddenly hear it everywhere?

Or when you're thinking about buying a certain car, you start seeing that model all the time?

That's your RAS in action—filtering reality to match what your mind is focused on. The same principle applies to your beliefs about yourself and the world. If you constantly tell yourself "I'll never succeed," your brain will tune into every failure, rejection, or struggle to reinforce that idea. But if you shift to "I am capable, and I'm improving every day," your brain will start noticing progress, opportunities, and strengths you previously ignored.

The Three Deep Breaths Method: Rewiring Your Mental Patterns

When a thought takes hold in your mind, it gathers momentum. The longer you focus on it, the stronger it becomes. But we can use this same principle to our advantage through a technique I call The *Three Deep Breaths Method*.

This works as a perfect complement to the *Pause & Pivot* technique you learned earlier. While *Pause & Pivot* helps you reset in moments of acute stress, the *Three Deep Breaths Method* allows you to systematically reprogram your deeper narrative patterns, creating lasting change in how you interpret your experiences.

Here's how it works:

1. With your first deep breath, clearly state your new narrative in your mind.

2. With your second breath, see yourself embodying this narrative in a specific situation.

3. With your third breath, feel the emotional shift this new story creates.

This cycle takes roughly 15-20 seconds and creates the mental space needed to interrupt old patterns. For maximum impact, repeat this cycle four times whenever possible, which creates enough sustained focus to begin shifting your biochemistry.

I experienced this transformation physically during a career-defining presentation. Standing backstage at the event venue, I felt my throat tightening, palms dampening with sweat. The murmur of the audience beyond the curtain only amplified my anxiety about stepping onto that stage. The familiar narrative—*"I'll forget something critical"*—had triggered my sympathetic nervous system, sending adrenaline coursing through my veins.

Instead of fighting the physical symptoms, I focused on my breathing, feeling the cool air entering my nostrils, filling my lungs, and then the warm release as I exhaled. With my first breath, I held the thought: *"I've prepared thoroughly and know this material deeply."*

As I continued, I noticed my shoulders softening, dropping away from my ears. With my second breath, I visualized: *"The audience wants me to succeed—they're here to learn, not criticize."* My jaw unclenched. By the third breath, I felt the confidence spreading from my chest to my fingertips as I focused on *"I communicate complex ideas with clarity and confidence."*

After repeating this cycle four times, my physiology had completely shifted. My breathing was deeper, my posture taller, my mind clearer. I wasn't just thinking different thoughts—my body had literally recalibrated to a new frequency.

This isn't mystical thinking—it's how our brains function. Persistent thoughts form neural pathways. The more we reinforce these pathways, the more automatic they become, ultimately creating what psychologists call our "default mode network"—the background operating system of our minds.

From the Training Room: The 30-Second Script Flip

When a negative thought loop takes hold, try this immediate pattern disruptor used by elite athletes:

1. Place your hand on your heart (physical touch grounds you in the present)

2. Take one deep breath while silently saying, *"This thought is not serving me"*

3. Ask yourself: *"What would someone who loves me say about this situation?"*

Answer the question aloud, using your name in the third person

Take another deep breath while visualizing this new perspective

This exercise takes just 30 seconds and can be done anywhere. The combination of physical touch, breathing, and third-person perspective creates instant cognitive distance from limiting narratives.

Rewriting the Impossible: Ashley Caldwell's Story

Remember Ashley Caldwell, the Olympic aerial skier? Her journey of shifting from recovery to rebuilding went far deeper than I initially shared.

Ashley was just 17 when her world shattered. Standing at the top of an aerials ramp, she launched down the in-run, hit the jump, and twisted through the air. Then came the landing—and with it, the sickening sensation of something gone wrong. The crack in her knee wasn't just a sound—it was a physical jolt that shot through her entire body. As she tumbled to a stop on the snow, the searing pain was accompanied by the first tendrils of doubt wrapping around her future.

This moment presented Ashley with a critical choice about the story she would tell herself. Would this be the beginning of the end—a tragic tale of potential cut short? Or would it be merely a challenging chapter in a larger story of triumph?

The universe wasn't done testing her resolve. Exactly a year later—on the same jump where her first injury occurred—she tore her other ACL in a fluke crash. The symmetry was almost cruel, but Ashley's response was transformative. While two full seasons vanished in rehabilitation rooms and doubt-filled nights, she made a decision: "I was determined to be the best rehab athlete in the world." This wasn't just recovery; this was deliberate rebuilding.

"People were like, 'Oh, she's done,'" Ashley told me, her voice steady despite the weight of the memory. "I'm my own biggest critic, and I was wondering if I could get back to where I was."

The moment that changed everything wasn't the injury, but a simple question from her physical therapist during those endless, boring leg extensions: "Are you rebuilding or just recovering?"

That distinction transformed her entire approach. "Recovering meant getting back to where I was. Rebuilding meant coming back stronger," Ashley explained. "From that moment on, every repetition wasn't about fixing something broken. It was about building something better."

Instead of accepting a script of limitation, Ashley deliberately rewrote her narrative. Her rehabilitation became her rewriting process, with each painful repetition reinforcing her new story: "I'm becoming stronger than I was before."

The challenges continued—a shin injury in 2016, shoulder surgery in 2017, a frightening wipeout at the 2018 Olympics—but her narrative remained consistent. By 2022, with four Olympics and five major injuries behind her, Ashley's story reached its climactic scene: Olympic gold in mixed team aerials.

That medal, glinting against a career of bruises, was her proof: she'd set herself up to win through the power of her chosen narrative.

Every setback comes with a choice: Will this be the end of your story or merely the complication that precedes your finest hour?

Beyond Achievement: How Your Narrative Shapes Your Entire Life

The stories we tell ourselves don't just impact what we achieve—they fundamentally alter how we experience life on every level.

Your Body Believes Your Stories

We saw in Chapter 3 how the housekeepers' bodies physically transformed once they changed their perception of their work. This same principle applies to our personal narratives on an even deeper level.

When we rehearse stories of victimhood, failure, or helplessness, our bodies release stress hormones like cortisol and adrenaline. Prolonged exposure to these chemicals compromise immune function, disrupts sleep patterns, and even accelerates cellular aging. This explains why individuals who continuously rehearse negative narratives often experience more frequent illness, chronic pain, and slower recovery from injury.

Conversely, empowering narratives trigger the release of oxytocin, dopamine, and endorphins—chemicals that reduce inflammation, enhance immune function, and accelerate healing. Ashley's physical resilience wasn't just about her training regimen—her narrative of "getting stronger through adversity" created a biochemical environment that supported her physical recovery.

Your Relationships Reflect Your Inner Story

The narratives we hold shape how we interact with others and, crucially, how they respond to us. When I was caught in my workplace resentment story, my relationships deteriorated in subtle ways —colleagues sensed my negativity and naturally created distance.

After shifting to a narrative of gratitude and opportunity, I noticed immediate changes in how people engaged with me. Conversations became more open, collaborative opportunities increased, and my network expanded. The external reality shifted to match my internal story.

Narrative Reframing in Action: Recognizing Value in Unexpected Places

In my current role at a global brand, I see firsthand how narrative reframing drives everything—from the pitches athletes deliver to the partnerships we choose to pursue.

Last year, a smaller, less established sports organization pitched us a partnership. My initial narrative could have easily been: "This probably isn't worth our investment—they don't have the reach or prestige of our typical partners." Had I allowed that story to take hold, I would have approached the meeting with diminished attention and lower expectations, likely missing valuable potential.

Instead, I consciously rewrote the script: "This organization might offer unique access to an emerging audience we haven't fully tapped into." This subtle shift changed everything—my attention during their presentation became more focused, my questions more thoughtful, and my ability to see creative possibilities sharper.

During the meeting, instead of mentally checking boxes of why it wouldn't work, I was actively connecting dots between their offerings and our brand objectives. The result? We structured an innovative partnership that delivered exceptional ROI and opened an entirely new market segment for our brand.

The narrative you choose determines not just how you feel about an opportunity, but whether you can even perceive its potential value in the first place.

Meeting People Where They Are

I believe we're always evolving, changing. But depending on your mindset or your perspective, are you moving forward or backward? It's easy to look at others and judge what they've done in the past, but what if they learn from their mistakes and changed and rewrote their own story to something better?

I always try to meet people where they're at in that moment. It's not always easy to do, especially if people have done you wrong. But I think it's important to build a relationship with the people or person that's in front of you, the person in that moment.

My life's roadmap is a perfect example. I spent decades in the production world, shooting, editing, producing, and now I work in the sports marketing industry with amazing athletes. My career is completely different than it was 10 years ago, and before that, it was completely different again. Even though I carry many of the same personality traits throughout my life, the way I think and feel is much different now than it was 20 years ago.

The stories we tell about ourselves and others aren't static—they can evolve. And recognizing this possibility for growth in both ourselves and others is one of the most powerful narrative shifts we can make.

Meeting people where they are means recognizing that their story is still being written—just like yours.

The Narrative Rewriting Process

Throughout my work with elite athletes—and in my own personal journey—I've developed a systematic approach to transforming limiting narratives. The Narrative Rewriting Process builds on two key elements: the mental resilience forged through consistent, small wins and the brain's ability to rewire itself through focused repetition. While the Resilience Scorecard sharpens mental toughness day by day, this process applies that same discipline to the stories you tell yourself—replacing self-doubt with self-direction.

1. Uncover Your Current Story

First, identify the current narrative running in your mind. These stories often hide in plain sight, disguised as "facts" about yourself or your situation. Common limiting stories include:

"I don't have what it takes to succeed at this level."

"I always freeze under pressure."

"My background prevents me from achieving what others can."

"It's too late for me to make a significant change."

Bring these narratives into the light by completing this sentence: "The story I've been telling myself about this situation is..."

2. Find the Exceptions

Our minds selectively filter information to reinforce existing beliefs. To disrupt this pattern, deliberately search for evidence that contradicts your limiting narrative.

When Ashley Caldwell believed her career might be over after multiple injuries, she found exceptions to that story: her successfully rehabilitated legs were stronger than before; other athletes had overcome similar setbacks; her technical understanding of aerial skiing had deepened during recovery.

List at least three pieces of evidence that challenge your current story. Remember, you're not looking for major contradictions—even small exceptions can crack open a limiting narrative.

3. Craft Your New Storyline

Using your exceptions as building blocks, craft a new narrative that serves your growth. This isn't about baseless positivity—it's about creating a more complete and empowering interpretation of reality.

Instead of: "I'm too inexperienced to lead this project." Try: "My fresh perspective brings valuable insights others might miss, and each challenge expands my leadership capabilities."

Your new storyline should acknowledge challenges while focusing on possibilities, resources, and growth potential.

4. Practice with the Three Deep Breaths Method

This is where transformation moves from concept to reality. When you catch your mind reverting to the old script, intentionally redirect to your new narrative using the *Three Deep Breaths Method* we explored earlier.

Repeat this practice four times throughout the day to create new neural pathways. The key is consistency—even brief practice sessions accumulate to create significant change over time.

5. Create a Supportive Cast

The narratives of those around you inevitably influence your own. Optimize your environment by:

Identifying "narrative allies" who naturally reinforce your new story

Spending more time with those who embody the mindset you're developing

Communicating your new narrative to trusted supporters

Creating appropriate boundaries with those who reinforce limiting stories

Ashley surrounded herself with coaches and teammates who spoke about "when" she would return to competition, not "if"—subtly reinforcing her comeback narrative every day.

6. Turn Setbacks into Plot Twists

In any compelling story, obstacles don't end the narrative—they advance it. Train yourself to automatically ask: "How might this challenge be setting me up for a breakthrough?"

This transformation of setbacks into plot twists is a powerful evolution of the "Rebuilding vs. Recovering" distinction we explored in Ashley's story. While that concept focused primarily on physical setbacks, we're now applying the same principle to our mental narratives—not just rebuilding from challenges, but using them to create a more compelling storyline.

When I lost a major client early in my career, I initially saw it as confirmation that I wasn't cut out for success. By reframing it as a necessary plot twist, I discovered it had freed my time and attention for the opportunity that ultimately launched my career to new heights.

Life will inevitably present setbacks. Your ability to immediately frame them as plot twists rather than conclusions will determine whether your story is a tragedy or a triumph.

The most courageous edit isn't changing what happened to you—it's changing the meaning you assign to it.

Rewriting Your Narrative: A Guided Transformation

You've already learned to apply the Resilience Scorecard to physical challenges and the Mental Forge techniques to cognitive growth. Now we're taking your implementation skills to a deeper level—reprogramming the very stories that define your identity and potential.

Take the next 15 minutes to work through this progressive exercise. Each step builds on the previous one, guiding you through the Narrative Rewriting Process in real-time.

Step 1: Identify Your Current Script

Think of an area where you feel stuck or limited. What's the narrative you've been telling yourself? Complete these sentences:

> In this situation, I believe I am...

> The story I tell myself about why this is happening is...

> I think this means that I can't...

> When I think about this, I feel...

Step 2: Uncover the Evidence Trail

Our minds build cases to support our existing beliefs. What "evidence" has your mind been collecting?

> List three specific experiences your mind uses as "proof" of your limiting narrative

> For each piece of evidence, write down how you've interpreted its meaning

> Notice any patterns in how you interpret events

Step 3: Find the Exceptions

Now, deliberately search for evidence that contradicts or complicates your limiting narrative:

When was a time, even briefly, when the opposite of your limiting belief was true?

Who has succeeded despite facing similar circumstances?

What strengths or resources do you have that your limiting narrative ignores?

If a friend told you they believed your limiting story about themselves, what evidence would you point to that contradicts it?

Step 4: Draft Your Rewrite

Using the exceptions you've identified, craft a new narrative that feels both truthful and empowering:

This situation is actually an opportunity for...

A more complete interpretation of what's happening is...

My strengths that will help me navigate this include...

The meaning I choose to assign to this experience is...

Step 5: Experience the Transformation

Let's experience the power of the *Three Deep Breaths Method* right now:

1. Take your first deep breath while clearly stating your new narrative

2. Take your second breath while visualizing yourself embodying this narrative

3. Take your third breath while feeling the emotional shift this creates

4. Repeat this cycle four times

5. Write down any shifts in your emotional state or physical sensations

Before & After Example:

BEFORE: "I'm too disorganized to succeed in leadership positions. Every time I take on more responsibility, details fall through the cracks. This proves I should stick to individual contributor roles where my weakness impacts fewer people."

EVIDENCE COLLECTED:

Missed a deadline on the Thompson project last year

Forgot to include two people on an important email chain

Got overwhelmed with the quarterly planning documents

EXCEPTIONS:

Successfully led the crisis response when the server crashed

Received positive feedback on my ability to keep the team focused on priorities

My "disorganization" sometimes allows me to make creative connections others miss

My colleague Michael has similar organizational challenges but has implemented systems that support his leadership role

AFTER: "I have natural strengths in creative thinking and big-picture vision that make me valuable in leadership roles. While detail management isn't my default setting, I can implement systems to support this area while leveraging my strengths. Each organizational challenge provides data on which supports I need to put in place. I'm developing as a leader who knows how to complement my natural abilities with strategic systems."

Overcoming Resistance: What to Expect

As you implement your new narrative, your mind will initially resist. This is normal! The old narrative has created neural pathways that won't disappear overnight. You might experience:

Intrusive thoughts reinforcing the old story

Physical discomfort when practicing the new narrative

"Yes, but..." thoughts that try to discredit your exceptions

Unconsciously seeking situations that confirm the old story

When you encounter resistance:

1. Acknowledge it without judgment ("There's that old story again")

2. Return to your exceptions list for reinforcement

3. Immediately implement the *Three Deep Breaths Method*

4. Remember that resistance indicates you're challenging the status quo—it's a sign of growth!

Your commitment to practicing your new narrative several times daily will gradually reduce resistance and establish new neural pathways. Within 30 days of consistent practice, you'll notice significant shifts in how naturally your new narrative comes to mind.

Final Challenge: Write the Next Scene

Take five minutes right now to describe the next chapter of your life as if it were already happening. Use present tense ("I am" not "I will") and vivid, specific details that engage all your senses.

Here's an example to inspire you:

"I am walking into the conference room with confident posture, feeling the smooth leather portfolio in my hands. The presentation materials inside are meticulously prepared. As I connect my laptop to the projector, I notice my breathing is calm and steady. My voice carries easily across the room as I begin, making eye contact with each decision-maker. I'm articulating complex ideas with clarity and answering questions thoughtfully. The energy in the room is engaged and receptive. As I conclude, I feel a surge of satisfaction, knowing I've communicated my vision effectively."

Now it's your turn. Write your next scene with the same level of sensory detail and present-moment awareness.

Your Mental Mastery Journey Continues

If life is 90% above the shoulders as we established at the beginning of our journey, then the stories you tell yourself represent the operating system running on that mental hardware. The previous chapters have helped you strengthen your mental capabilities—now we're focusing on the narratives that determine how those capabilities are applied.

From this moment forward, you are not just a character in your story.

You are the screenwriter, the director, and the star of your own narrative. The stories you tell yourself are setting you up either to win or to lose. Choose wisely.

While you now have the tools to rewrite your core narratives, you'll still face moments when negative thought patterns threaten to pull you back into old stories. In the next chapter, we'll explore specific techniques to break these loops before they can undermine your new narrative.

The screenplay of your life doesn't write itself. Either you pick up the pen, or your fears, past experiences, and other people's expectations will write it for you.

CHAPTER 5: THE SECRET TO BEATING NEGATIVE THOUGHT LOOPS

So far, we've built a progressive system for mental mastery—layer by layer.

We started with resilience, the foundation for persistence under pressure.

We forged cognitive strength through deliberate challenge.

We learned to take control of our mindset instead of letting it control us.

And we began rewriting the narratives that limit us.

Now, we add a fifth layer: the thought pattern debugging system—the tool that breaks the negative loops sabotaging your progress.

The Moment Everything Vanished: A Lesson in Mental Resilience

The cursor blinked once, twice—then nothing.

One moment, my manuscript existed—weeks of research, insights, and hard-earned wisdom living inside my laptop. The next moment, my screen went black before reopening to display the most terrifying sight any writer can imagine: a blank document.

No warning. No autosave notification. No recovery option.

Just... emptiness.

The pounding in my chest echoed in my ears as a cold wave of dread washed through me. I frantically searched for recovery files, temporary folders—anything that might contain fragments of my work. Nothing. The manuscript for *Above the Shoulders* had vanished into the digital void.

And of course, this happened at 9:47 p.m. on the Friday of a holiday weekend. No IT support. No rescue coming. Just me, my betrayal of a laptop, and the crushing weight of loss—a perfect test of whether I truly believed what I was writing about, that what happens above the shoulders determines everything else in life.

My reaction was testing every resilience principle I had worked so hard to build. Just as I'd used *Bite-Sized Wins* to conquer that impossible desert dune with "three more steps," I now needed to break this overwhelming setback into manageable pieces I could tackle. The mental resilience that carried me through physical challenges was about to face a different kind of test—one happening entirely above the shoulders.

How Mental Loops Begin

My mind immediately launched into what neuroscientists call a catastrophic thought cascade:

"I've lost everything." (The initial trigger)

"Months of work, gone forever." (The amplification)

"I'll never recover what I had." (The generalization)

"This is a sign I shouldn't be writing this book." (The false meaning-making)

Each thought linked to the next like falling dominoes, each one knocking down my confidence a little more. This is precisely how negative thought loops hijack your brain—they don't just make you feel bad; they systematically dismantle your ability to see possibilities.

Negative thought loops are like being stuck on a mental treadmill—expending enormous energy without moving forward. You're running harder and harder, heart pounding, sweat pouring, but you're not actually getting anywhere. You're just wearing yourself out while staring at the same wall of worry. The exhaustion is real, but the distance covered is zero.

I could almost feel what was happening inside my head. My amygdala—the brain's emotional alarm system—had seized control, flooding my system with cortisol and adrenaline. Meanwhile, my prefrontal cortex—the rational, problem-solving command center—was being systematically suppressed.

This mental ambush perfectly illustrated how neuroplasticity can work against you. Instead of strengthening helpful pathways—like the ones that powered London's cab drivers—my negative thought cascade was reinforcing the ones that made me feel helpless. My prefrontal cortex—my brain's command center—was being overridden by the amygdala's emergency signals.

Neuroscientists call this an "amygdala hijack," and it's the biological foundation of every spiral into negativity.

The laptop screen stared back at me, blank and indifferent to my crisis. I stared back, caught in the grip of thoughts I couldn't control. This mental ambush—happening entirely above the shoulders—was determining how I experienced this crisis more than the crisis itself.

The Pivotal Question

I sat there, coffee growing cold in my hands, heartbeat gradually slowing from panic to resignation. The negative loop had nearly won.

Then, from somewhere deeper than conscious thought, a different question surfaced:

"What if this isn't the end of something, but the beginning?"

The question didn't come with fanfare. It wasn't a lightning bolt of inspiration. It was quieter, like a whisper you almost miss but can't unhear once you've caught it.

And here's the truth that changed everything: I hadn't lost the essence; I'd only lost the words.

The research still lived in my mind. The insights I'd gained through interviews, study, and personal experience remained intact. The core message—that resilience is built above the shoulders first—was still mine to share.

I hadn't lost my book. I'd lost one draft of it.

In that moment, I understood viscerally what I'd been writing about intellectually: how we interpret events—not the events themselves—determines their impact on us. My entire experience of this crisis was about to be transformed by a single shift above the shoulders.

The Moment of Reframing

This is where something remarkable happened—something I only later realized was part of a deeper system I'd been building all along.

Pause & Pivot helps reset in moments of acute stress. Narrative rewriting reshapes your identity at the root. But what we're doing here? This is about disrupting the loops—those thought spirals that repeat, intensify, and sabotage progress.

This is the mental debugging system. The one that hits the emergency stop on that mental treadmill and moves you to an entirely different track.

I consciously reframed the situation:

Old frame: "This crash is a disaster that has destroyed my work."

New frame: "This crash is a challenge that will improve my work."

The circumstances hadn't changed. The lost manuscript was still lost. But by shifting the frame—the mental context through which I interpreted the event—I completely transformed its meaning and its impact on me.

As I opened a fresh document and typed the first few words, I felt a surge of energy that hadn't been present before. Ideas flowed with unexpected clarity. Concepts I'd struggled to articulate suddenly found their perfect expression. Connections between ideas emerged that I hadn't seen in the original draft.

By midnight, I turned to my wife and said something that surprised even me: "I think this version is better than what I lost."

She smiled knowingly. "It's almost like you needed to lose it to find what you were really trying to say."

The Neuroscience of the Shift: What's Happening Above the Shoulders

This shift in my brain during reframing is a real-time example of how neuroplasticity works. Just like London cab drivers reshape their brains through deliberate mental effort, we can redirect neural activity from the amygdala to the prefrontal cortex—turning panic into clarity through conscious reframing.

Imagine your brain as a landscape with two major cities. The Amygdala City is where emotions run high and perspective narrows.

Prefrontal Cortex City is where rational thought, creative problem-solving, and strategic thinking happen.

When you're caught in a negative thought loop, all traffic is being directed to Amygdala City, causing gridlock and chaos. Reframing is like opening an alternate route that diverts traffic back to Prefrontal Cortex City, restoring order and functionality to your mental landscape.

This isn't just psychological theory. Using fMRI technology, neuroscientists have actually observed this shift in brain activity when people successfully reframe negative situations. You're literally changing which parts of your brain are driving your behavior.

The Three Most Destructive Mental Traps

Before we dive deeper into the solutions, let's identify the most common negative thought patterns that keep people stuck:

1. Catastrophizing—Expecting the worst possible outcome from any challenging situation

Example: When my manuscript disappeared, my first thought wasn't "I'll need to rewrite some sections"—it was "My entire book is ruined and I'll never recover."

2. Overgeneralization—Taking one negative event and applying it to your entire life

Example: From "I lost this document" to "I always lose important things" or "Nothing ever works out for me."

3. Rumination—Continuously dwelling on problems without taking constructive action

Example: Replaying the moment of loss over and over, imagining different scenarios where I had backed up the file, but never actually moving toward a solution.

These patterns don't just make you feel bad momentarily—they rewire your brain for negativity. According to a study published in the Journal of Behavioral Medicine, chronic negative rumination is linked to higher levels of cortisol, the stress hormone, which can impair cognitive function and exacerbate feelings of despair. This creates a biological feedback loop that makes it increasingly difficult to break free.

Pause here. Think of a recent moment when your mind spun out of control. Was it catastrophizing ("This ruins everything")? Overgeneralizing ("I always fail")? Or ruminating ("I can't stop replaying this")? Jot it down—naming it is the first step to taming it.

The Research Behind Reframing

As my dad would say, "Sports is 80% above the shoulders"—a wisdom that became the foundation for this book's core message that life itself is 90% above the shoulders. When it comes to breaking negative thought loops, this isn't just folk wisdom; it's backed by decades of research into how our mental processes determine our outcomes.

Dr. Martin Seligman's research on optimistic explanatory styles shows that people who view negative events as temporary, specific, and external rather than permanent, universal, and personal are significantly more resilient to stress and setbacks. This approach isn't about denying reality—it's about interpreting it in a way that empowers rather than paralyzes you.

This is precisely what I did when I reframed my manuscript disaster —I viewed it as a temporary, specific challenge rather than a permanent, universal failure.

As Nelson Mandela demonstrated through his extraordinary life, "The greatest glory in living lies not in never falling, but in rising every time we fall." After 27 years of imprisonment, he emerged not bitter but resolute, having transformed what could have been a dungeon of resentment into a forge for his leadership. His mindset—his ability to reframe his circumstances above the shoulders—didn't just change his personal experience; it changed the trajectory of a nation.

The 60-Second Loop Breaker

Before we go further, let me give you something you can use immediately—a quick exercise I call the "Loop Breaker" that can snap you out of negative thought patterns in just 60 seconds. Think of it as your emergency stop button for that mental treadmill:

1. Change your posture—sit up straighter or stand if you can.

2. Shake out your arms like you're flinging off tension.

3. Take a deep breath and say (even if just in your head): *"This loop stops now—I'm taking back control."*

4. Look around and physically acknowledge three things that are working in your favor right now.

This might sound simple, but it works because it combines movement with a conscious mental reset. I've used this technique everywhere—from long flights to stressful meetings to moments of self-doubt before big decisions. It's my emergency brake for runaway negative thinking.

Try it now. I'll wait.

The Impatience Trap: Reframing Everyday Annoyances

Let's get real for a minute: I'm not a saint when it comes to patience. Take driving, for instance. Nothing gets under my skin faster than someone cruising in the passing lane like they're on a scenic tour, oblivious to the line of cars behind them.

For years, I'd stew in that frustration, convinced these people were just self-absorbed. I'd mutter to myself, *"Don't they get how their actions mess with everyone else?"* But here's the thing: that irritation wasn't just a passing annoyance—it was a full-on negative thought loop. I'd catastrophize: *"This is ruining my whole day!"* I'd overgeneralize: *"Why is everyone so clueless?"* And then I'd ruminate, replaying the moment in my head like a bad movie on repeat.

Sound familiar? That's the mental treadmill in action. I was sprinting nowhere, working myself into a lather over something I couldn't control, all while my blood pressure climbed and my mood plummeted. It's exhausting, and it all happens right up here, above the shoulders—in the battlefield of our minds where life's true quality is determined.

Then I stumbled onto a little trick. Now, when I catch myself spiraling, I imagine those slow drivers are tourists, wide-eyed and soaking in the sights. Maybe they're lost in wonder, or maybe they're just *really* curious about that storefront. It's hard to stay mad at that. I've been that tourist, marveling at something new, oblivious to the chaos I might be causing.

What's really helped me level up is asking myself: *"If I didn't know why this person was acting this way, would it look silly to get worked up?"* Maybe that slow driver had a bad experience and feels safest in the left lane. Who knows? The point is, I don't. And I don't need to.

Here's the kicker: I can't control what they do—but I *can* control what I think and how I feel. When I reframe it, I'm not just saving my sanity—I'm rewiring my brain.

Your brain constantly filters experience based on your beliefs and expectations. During negative thought loops, this filtering mechanism goes into overdrive, creating a downward spiral where your mind selectively attends to evidence supporting your negative perspective while filtering out contradictory information.

If I expect people to be selfish, that's all I'll see. But if I look for curiosity or innocence instead, my mind starts spotting it. It's like tuning my mental radio to a better station.

I was in Nashville last year, stuck behind a driver going precisely 5 mph under the speed limit. My blood pressure was climbing when I forced myself to try this reframe. "They're probably just enjoying the skyline view," I told myself. As we approached a stoplight, I pulled up beside them and glanced over—it was an elderly couple, the woman pointing excitedly at buildings while her husband nodded, both with expressions of pure wonder. They were tourists, just as I'd imagined. That moment of confirmation transformed how I approach similar situations.

So here's my challenge to you: next time you're stuck behind a dawdling driver or weaving around a sidewalk roadblock, try this. Picture them as tourists or curious explorers. See if it shifts your mood. If you crack a smile—or at least stop grinding your teeth— that's your mind taking the wheel. Small win, big impact.

The Utah Winter Reframe: Finding Joy in What You Despise

I once saw Utah winters as nothing but months of misery wrapped in white. Living on the bench of the Wasatch Mountains, every snowfall felt like a personal attack. The Wasatch Front gets hammered with an average of 500 inches of snow annually at its ski resorts, and even where I lived at 4,600 feet elevation, we'd still see 50-100 inches a year.

Every time it snowed, and I had to shovel, I'd feel my blood boil. A foot of fresh powder meant an hour of back-breaking labor, and my thought loop was simple but powerful:

"This weather is terrible." "I hate shoveling." "Utah winters are ruining my quality of life."

One morning, after an especially unrelenting storm dropped nearly two feet overnight, I stood in my driveway at 5:30 AM, leaning on my shovel and watching my breath form clouds in the freezing air. My neighbor was cheerfully clearing his own driveway, whistling as he worked. I must have looked miserable because he called over, "Beautiful morning, isn't it?" I thought he was being sarcastic until I saw his genuine smile.

"How can you possibly enjoy this?" I asked.

"Are you kidding?" he said, gesturing at the mountains. "Fresh powder! I'm heading up to Snowbird as soon as I'm done here. Best skiing of the season!"

That moment was my first clue that my hatred of winter wasn't inevitable—it was a choice happening above my shoulders.

While my wakesurfing journey showed how a growth mindset can turn failure into feedback, this snow story reveals something different —how we can completely invert our emotional relationship with ongoing challenges through deliberate perspective shifts.

I realized I had two choices: continue this battle against immovable forces of nature, or find a way to reframe my relationship with winter entirely. The pivotal question that changed everything came unexpectedly: "What if I could actually look forward to snow instead of dreading it?"

So, I threw myself into skiing—full throttle, no half-measures.

From that moment, everything flipped. My negative thought loop transformed into excitement and anticipation. I couldn't wait for it to snow, and the more it snowed, the better. Even shoveling became a twisted kind of foreplay to the slopes—each scoop of snow no longer representing burden but possibility. What was once drudgery became preparation for joy, like setting the table before a feast.

The remarkable thing wasn't just the shift in my mood—it was how completely my reality changed through this simple reframing. The snow hadn't changed. The work hadn't changed. My physical location hadn't changed. The only thing that changed was how I chose to interpret these circumstances.

Notice how once I reframed snow as positive, I began seeking out snow reports, celebrating big storms, and finding evidence that supported my new perspective—a perfect real-world example of redirecting confirmation bias to serve rather than sabotage us. Rather than cherry-picking evidence of winter's hardships, my mind now eagerly collected proof of winter's gifts.

Your Winter: What's your equivalent of Utah winters—something in your life you currently resent but could potentially reframe? Is it your commute? A difficult work relationship? Family obligations? What potential joy or meaning might be hidden within this challenge if you shifted your perspective above the shoulders?

The Three Keys to Breaking Negative Thought Loops

Building on the mental tools we've developed in previous chapters, my manuscript disaster revealed three specialized strategies for breaking negative thought patterns—each one representing the next evolution of our above-the-shoulders mastery:

1. Recognition is the essential first step

Before you can break a negative thought loop, you must recognize you're in one. The moment I became aware of my catastrophic thinking pattern about the lost manuscript, I gained the power to intervene.

Your practice: When facing a setback, pause and ask, "Am I in a thought loop right now, or am I seeing this situation clearly?" This moment of metacognition—thinking about your thinking—creates space for change.

2. Reframing isn't denial; it's perspective-shifting

I didn't pretend losing my work wasn't painful. I didn't tell myself it didn't matter. Instead, I changed how I interpreted its meaning and its implications for my future.

Your practice: When confronting a challenge, ask yourself: "What else could this mean? What opportunity might be hiding within this problem?" Finding an alternative meaning is the heart of reframing.

3. Action dissolves anxiety, even when the action is small

Opening a new document and writing the first sentence was a tiny step, but it broke the paralysis of negative thinking. Action sends a powerful signal to your brain that you're not helpless.

This action principle is the tactical version of the *Bite-Sized Wins* strategy. That desert race taught me to focus on just "three more steps" in the face of physical overwhelm—here, we're using the same approach to tackle mental paralysis. One small action. One forward step. That's how you break the cycle of overthinking.

Your practice: Identify one small, immediate action you can take in response to any setback. Don't worry about solving the entire problem—just take the first step to prove to yourself that movement is possible.

Your Turn: Breaking Your Own Loops

Think about a recent setback that sent your thoughts spiraling. Now trace the exact path your thinking followed:

What was the initial trigger thought?

How did it escalate into a loop?

What meaning did you assign to the event?

How did that meaning affect your ability to respond effectively?

Now, try reframing the situation. If you had approached that same event with the mindset that challenges reveal opportunities, what different meaning could you have assigned to it? What different actions might you have taken?

I remember coaching a friend through this exercise after she was passed over for a promotion she'd worked toward for years. Her initial thoughts followed a familiar pattern:

"I was overlooked again." (Trigger) "They'll never recognize my contributions." (Escalation) "I'm not valued at this company." (Meaning-making) "Maybe I'm just not good enough." (False conclusion)

This mental script left her paralyzed, unable to advocate for herself or see alternatives—she was stuck on that mental treadmill, running hard but going nowhere. But when we reframed the situation—"This isn't a permanent rejection; it's information about what skills I need to develop next"—everything shifted. She stepped off the treadmill of negative rumination and onto a path of actual progress. Within three months, she'd enrolled in a certification program, had a candid conversation with her manager about her career path, and was heading up a new initiative that eventually led to an even better position than the one she'd initially wanted.

Remember, you can't always control what happens, but you always control the story you tell yourself about what happened. And that story determines everything that follows.

Moving Forward: From Negative Loops to Goal Achievement

The tools in this chapter complete your mental mastery foundation. You now have a full toolkit—resilience to persist, strength forged through challenge, control over your mindset, the ability to rewrite limiting narratives, and the power to escape negative thought loops.

With those psychological foundations in place, you're ready to shift from preparation to application. What's next? Goal-setting and mental focus—turning all this inner work into real-world outcomes. The mental infrastructure you've built isn't just about feeling better; it's about doing what once felt impossible. Now it's time to aim higher —and learn how to hit your target.

This is the ultimate secret to breaking free from negative thought loops: recognizing that every crisis carries within it the seeds of opportunity, waiting for a mindset strong enough to nurture them.

The blank screen that once represented my greatest writing disaster became the catalyst for writing the best version of this book. The very chapter you're reading now—on breaking negative thought patterns —was strengthened by my firsthand battle with exactly that challenge.

The mental treadmill isn't just a metaphor—it's a trap millions find themselves in daily. Breaking negative thought loops is like hitting the emergency stop button, stepping off completely, and redirecting that same energy toward actual forward movement. While the treadmill burns calories without changing your location, taking that same effort outside means each step carries you toward a destination. Reframing is exactly this shift—transforming mental energy that once kept you stuck into a force that propels you forward.

Your mind is now prepared for the next level. Let's put it to work.

Remember, as we've explored throughout this chapter, everything meaningful in life happens first above the shoulders. Your thoughts shape your reality in ways both subtle and profound. When you master the art of breaking negative thought loops, you're not just improving your mental state—you're fundamentally changing how you experience and interact with the world. This is the true power of living from above the shoulders: the ability to transform your external reality by first transforming your internal landscape.

PART II

TRAINING YOUR MIND FOR SUCCESS (HOWEVER YOU DEFINE IT)

CHAPTER 6: THE SCIENCE OF GOAL-SETTING AND MENTAL FOCUS

You've built the mental infrastructure: resilience, cognitive strength, mindset control, empowering narratives, and freedom from negative thought loops.

Now it's time to channel that system into something tangible.

This is where mental mastery shifts from preparation to application —the moment when what's above the shoulders begins to manifest real-world results.

My fingers hovered over the "purchase" button on the fitness app. A familiar battle raged above my shoulders—a burst of excitement colliding with the quiet certainty that this initial rush would fade within days.

"This time will be different," whispered the optimist in my head. "I'll stick with it for the full 12 weeks and transform my body."

"Sure you will," countered the realist. "Just like the last three programs you bought. You'll use it for a week, then it'll join your digital grave-yard of abandoned self-improvement tools."

The truth hit me like a thunderbolt: It wasn't that I didn't want results badly enough. It was that I had been relying on motivation—that fickle, fair-weather friend—rather than developing the mental systems and focus that actually drive achievement.

This realization transformed not just my approach to fitness, but how I pursue every meaningful goal in my life. What happens above the shoulders—how we structure our thinking, focus our minds, and design our systems—determines what happens below them. It is the difference between dreams that dissolve and achievements that endure.

Why Mental Focus Beats Motivation Every Time

Retired Team Canada beach volleyball pro Sam Pedlow understands this better than most. Having competed at the highest levels and ranked in the global top 10, I first met Sam during a sponsor event where his intensity immediately stood out. Six-foot-six with shoulders like a linebacker, Sam's physical presence was imposing enough, but it was the focus in his eyes that really struck me.

When we connected later for coffee and I asked him about maintaining intensity through grueling seasons, his answer surprised me: "I'm not motivated every day. Not even close."

He leaned forward, his eyes intense with conviction that almost made me lean back in my chair. "There are mornings when every muscle aches like I've been hit by a truck, when the sand looks too hot to touch, when my body is screaming at me to take a day off. But I've built a system that doesn't depend on how I feel."

Sam laughed, rubbing the calluses on his hands—battle scars from thousands of practice dives. "Last month in Brazil, I woke up with food poisoning the day of a crucial match. Spent half the night in the bathroom. My motivation level was zero—actually, it was negative. But my system kicked in: 15-minute mobility routine, visualization sequence, match-day nutrition protocol—adjusted for the circumstances. We won that match because my body was on autopilot even when my mind wanted nothing to do with volleyball."

What humanizes Sam's approach even further is how he builds flexibility into his discipline. "Look, I know there will be setbacks, but with my 80/20 approach, they're already baked into the plan," he explained. "My wife loves pizza, so I know I'll enjoy a slice every once in a while because it's something we like to do together. I don't make it a habit since my other goals keep me eating a specific way, but I also don't want to eliminate those moments of connection when we go out together."

This approach turns conventional wisdom on its head. We're taught to chase motivation—to find inspiration in transformation videos, motivational speeches, or visualization boards. Yet professional athletes like Sam don't rely on these temporary bursts of enthusiasm. They build systems that generate consistent action regardless of emotional state.

Research shows that motivation naturally fluctuates based on dozens of variables—sleep quality, stress levels, blood sugar, recent wins or losses. Relying on motivation means surrendering your goals to those shifting conditions.

Mental focus works differently. When you systematize your approach, you shift the workload from your emotional centers to your prefrontal cortex—the part of your brain built for planning, execution, and long-term success.

What system are you currently using to achieve your goals? Or are you still counting on motivation to carry you through? Let me share how I learned the power of systems over inspiration through an unexpected collaboration that transformed my approach to achievement.

The Power of Breaking It Down: How We Created Our First Short Film

Early in my career as a video editor, I had a long-standing desire to create a short film. I imagined how it could propel my career, serve as a submission to film festivals, and teach me invaluable lessons about storytelling and production. The idea lingered in my mind for years —exciting but overwhelming.

Then, everything changed when my best friend—who worked in the same industry—proposed that we collaborate on a project. Unlike me, he had a structured approach to tackling ambitious goals. He already had a script and a vision for how to bring it to life.

"You've been talking about making a film for years," he challenged me. "Are you ever going to make it, or just keep talking?"

His question stung because it was true. But instead of just criticizing, he took the reins and showed me how to build a system to turn this dream into reality. We methodically broke down "making a film" into discrete components: refining his script, blocking out weekly work sessions, scouting locations, and assembling a team. Instead of waiting for creative inspiration, we committed to specific production milestones with deadlines.

One moment stands out—filming in an abandoned jail after being denied by five other facilities. Standing in that cold, concrete cell with equipment failing and the schedule slipping, I felt panic creeping in. My mind raced with visions of the entire project collapsing. But rather than letting it overwhelm me, my friend nudged me and said, "Just focus on fixing the lights for now."

That simple redirection to the immediate next step pulled me out of paralysis. I took a deep breath, adjusted the gels on our main light, repositioned the bounce card, and suddenly the scene came to life. The harsh shadows softened, revealing details in the cell that told a story on their own. That small victory—solving just one specific problem—gave me the mental space to tackle the next challenge, and the next.

This micro-focus approach—zeroing in on the next actionable step rather than the entire mountain—became my blueprint for tackling any big goal.

It's like when I was learning to wakesurf. Instead of obsessing over the full 360-degree spin that had eluded me for two summers, I broke it down into specific components: weight distribution, shoulder rotation, eye focus. Each piece became a manageable challenge—one I could improve—rather than getting overwhelmed by the trick as a whole.

When our film was complete, we rented a theater to show it to our family, friends, and everyone who had helped make it possible. The feeling of watching something we had created together come to life on the big screen was indescribable—a tangible reward for our systematic approach that eventually led to festival success.

That moment—when I realized breaking an overwhelming goal into manageable chunks could transform the impossible into the inevitable—might just be the missing piece in your own journey too.

The Complete Achievement System: Three Essential Components

Throughout my work with elite performers and through my own journey of transformation, I've discovered that achievement isn't about following a rigid multi-step program. Instead, it's about integrating three essential components that work together to create a complete system. Let's explore each of these components and how they combine to turn impossible goals into inevitable outcomes.

Component 1: Internal Blueprint - The Power of Visualization

Visualization isn't just positive thinking—it's structured mental rehearsal. It builds on the Mental Movie Method and the Next Scene Writing technique, transforming imagination into a tool for performance.

Those earlier techniques helped reprogram your mindset and narrative. This advanced approach targets achievement directly. Breaking down goals creates external structure; visualization builds the internal framework. Together, they form a system that works from the inside out and the outside in.

When I interviewed freestyle skier Ashley Caldwell about how she prepares for impossibly complex aerial maneuvers, she described a sophisticated process that extends far beyond simple positive imagery.

"I don't just see myself doing the trick," she explained. "I feel every rotation, sense the exact moment to initiate each twist, and experience the landing impact—all while standing still. My body is literally learning through my mind."

This isn't just athlete talk—it's science. Your brain can't tell the difference between a vividly imagined experience and reality. Studies confirm it: athletes who visualize activate the same neural pathways as physical practice.

Remember those London cab drivers? The same neuroplasticity applies to visualization. When you mentally rehearse with detail, you literally create new neural pathways—just like those cabbies who expanded their brain's navigational centers through focused practice.

I've watched Ashley standing motionless at the top of a jump, eyes closed, hands subtly mimicking movements. To an outsider, it might look like she's lost her mind, standing there twitching slightly while everyone else is physically preparing. In reality, she's programming success patterns directly into her brain—a technique that's just as applicable to your next presentation, project launch, or difficult conversation as it is to her Olympic-level skiing.

The most effective visualization includes several key elements:

Specificity: See the exact moment of success in vivid detail

Sensory immersion: Feel the physical sensations, hear the sounds, notice the smells

Emotional connection: Experience the pride, joy, and satisfaction of achievement

Process focus: Visualize not just the outcome, but the steps to get there

Consistency: Practice daily to strengthen neural pathways

How different would your approach to goals be if you spent five minutes each morning mentally rehearsing both the process and outcome of success with this level of detail? What happens above the shoulders—in those five minutes of focused mental rehearsal—could transform everything that happens below them.

Component 2: Strategic Approaches - Lessons from Elite Performers

Elite performers like Ashley Caldwell and Sam Pedlow have developed complementary approaches to goal achievement that form the second component of our system. Their methods reveal powerful insights about progression and sustainability that we can apply to any meaningful goal.

Ashley's Progressive Approach

Ashley Caldwell's journey has already taught us powerful lessons—from her rebuilding-versus-recovering mindset to the way she reshaped her personal narrative. Now, she reveals a third dimension of her mental mastery.

"In freestyle skiing, progression is everything," Ashley explained during one of our sponsor events. "You don't just decide to do a quadruple-twisting triple backflip. You build up to it systematically, with clear benchmarks along the way."

From Ashley, we learn the importance of starting with a clear vision of your ultimate goal, then breaking it down into skill components that can be mastered separately. She creates a progressive training ladder with increasingly difficult sub-goals that build upon each other. While keeping the outcome in mind, she focuses daily attention on the controllable actions that lead to those outcomes, tracking specific metrics that provide concrete feedback on her progress.

What makes Ashley's approach so powerful is how it transforms overwhelming goals into manageable challenges through systematic progression—the same principle I discovered during our short film project.

Sam's Sustainability System

While Ashley focuses on progression, Sam Pedlow has mastered the art of sustainability. His approach ensures that progress continues even when motivation fails or life throws unexpected challenges your way.

"The biggest mistake I see in goal pursuit is the all-or-nothing mentality," Sam shared over coffee after an early morning training session. "People create these perfect but unsustainable systems. When they inevitably slip up, they abandon everything."

From Sam, we learn the power of the 80/20 rule—maintaining strict discipline in 80% of your habits while allowing 20% flexibility for balance and sustainability. He focuses on consistency rather than perfection, measures what actually drives results rather than vanity metrics, and creates weekly rhythms rather than expecting every day to be perfect.

Sam builds accountability systems that catch him when willpower fails and prioritizes recovery as an essential component of sustainable performance. "Willpower fails eventually," he emphasized, his eyes revealing the cost of lessons learned the hard way. "You need systems that hold you accountable when motivation inevitably dips."

Together, Ashley and Sam's approaches create a powerful strategic framework that combines progressive skill development with sustainable implementation—a perfect foundation for turning any impossible goal into an inevitable outcome.

Component 3: Practical Implementation - Bringing It All Together

The final component is where vision meets action—the practical implementation system that turns mental rehearsal and strategic frameworks into daily progress. This component creates the bridge between what happens above the shoulders and what happens in the real world.

An effective implementation system includes three core elements:

1. Clarity

Transform vague aspirations into specific outcomes with measurable metrics and hard deadlines. Anchor your goal to a meaningful "why" that will power you through tough days.

2. Progression

Create a systematic ladder of achievement with sequential milestones that build upon each other. Break overwhelming challenges into specific weekly actions that feel manageable rather than intimidating.

3. Consistency

Design a daily process with specific actions that drive progress, build in flexibility to prevent all-or-nothing thinking, track your progress visually to generate momentum, and schedule regular review sessions to adjust your approach based on real-world feedback.

Let me show you how these three elements work together in real life with the story of a friend who went from kitchen clueless to culinary competent in just 90 days.

The System in Action: From Kitchen Clueless to a Birthday Feast in 90 Days

Picture a friend of mine who couldn't tell a spatula from a soup ladle. For years, he'd nod along as his wife raved about her favorite meal: her mom's creamy chicken Alfredo with garlic bread and a chocolate lava cake. He'd always say, "I'll make that for you someday." But "someday" never came—until he decided her birthday, three months away, was the deadline. He had zero cooking skills, but he knew nailing this would light up her world.

His initial goal was vague: "Cook something special for my wife some-day." Here's how he transformed it into an inevitable outcome using our three core implementation elements:

Clarity in Action:

He defined a specific outcome: "Prepare creamy chicken Alfredo, garlic bread, and chocolate lava cake for my wife's birthday on June 15th, good enough that she doesn't secretly order takeout."

He anchored it to his 'why': To see her face glow with that rare mix of shock and delight. This deeper motivation would power his system through tough days.

His recipe cards had notes in the margins about his wife's preferences —extra garlic in the bread, more chocolate in the cake. He'd even practiced describing each dish out loud to lock in his understanding. That clarity turned his daydream into a mission.

Progression in Action:

He created sequential milestones that built upon each other:

Master boiling pasta without it becoming a glue ball by week 3

Create a creamy Alfredo sauce by week 6

Bake edible garlic bread by week 9

Nail a gooey lava cake by week 11

Cook the full meal for a test run by week 12

For each milestone, he created more granular weekly targets. For the Alfredo sauce, he spent one week just learning to make a basic roux without burning it, another practicing the proper consistency, and a third balancing the flavors. This approach turned the intimidating task of "mastering Alfredo sauce" into specific weekly actions he could easily tackle.

Consistency in Action:

He identified three daily actions that would drive progress:

Practice cooking for 30 minutes five days a week

Watch one instructional cooking video daily

Review recipes and make shopping lists with his morning coffee

He built in flexibility by focusing on weekly consistency rather than daily perfection. If he missed a day, he'd use the 'Next Play Rule': no dwelling on the miss, just focus on the next step. This flexibility saved him when a work project demanded late hours one week. Instead of abandoning his plan entirely, he adjusted, combined practice sessions, and kept moving forward.

He tracked progress visually with a chart on his fridge. Every time he succeeded at a component—didn't burn the garlic bread or made a sauce worth tasting—he checked it off with a bold green marker. "Seeing those checkmarks stack up is weirdly addictive," he told me. "On days when I'm exhausted and don't feel like cooking, that chart pulls me into the kitchen anyway."

Every Sunday evening, he reviewed his progress. When obstacles hit —a sauce that kept breaking or a lava cake that refused to "lava"—he treated them as data, not failure. Week four's review revealed his sauce kept breaking because he added cream too quickly on high heat. In week nine, he discovered his oven temperature was off by 25 degrees. A $12 thermometer solved the garlic bread inconsistency problem.

The Results:

On her birthday—90 days from his "spatula, what's that?" baseline— he set the table, dimmed the lights, and served up creamy Alfredo, crispy garlic bread, and a lava cake that actually oozed.

She didn't just eat it. She asked for seconds. Then teared up. "You did this for me?"

When I asked what made the difference after years of empty promises, his answer hit home:

"I was terrified every time I turned on the stove. But the system didn't care about my nerves—it just kept me going. Breaking it into steps made it feel less like a mountain and more like a recipe I could follow."

The fears, doubts, and negative thought loops didn't disappear. The system just cooked right through them.

Have you ever noticed how some people seem to achieve goals effortlessly while others struggle despite working harder? It's rarely about natural talent or luck—it's almost always about having a superior mental framework for achievement. The system above your shoulders determines the results below them.

Your Complete Mental Achievement System: The Integration

When we combine these three components—the internal visualization blueprint, the strategic approaches of progression and sustainability, and the practical implementation system—we create a comprehensive approach that addresses every dimension of achievement:

1. **Visualization** creates the neural pathways that make success feel inevitable

2. **Strategic Approaches** balance progression with sustainability to ensure continued growth

3. **Implementation** transforms ideas into action through clarity, progression, and consistency

This isn't just another collection of tips and tricks; it's a cohesive system where each component reinforces the others. The visualization primes your brain for action; the strategic approaches provide the roadmap; and the implementation system creates the daily progress that turns dreams into reality.

In essence, we're building a mental operating system that turns impossible goals into inevitable outcomes—not through motivation or willpower, but through systematic application of what happens above the shoulders.

From Insight to Action

The difference between those who achieve their goals and those who merely wish for them isn't talent or luck—it's the systematic application of mental focus in service of clear objectives. Remember that impossible goal you identified in the Introduction? The one that seemed beyond reach? Now that you've built a complete mental achievement system, let's apply these principles to transform it from distant dream to inevitable achievement.

Your Turn: 15-Minute Implementation

Take the next 15 minutes right now to apply this system to your impossible goal. Don't just read about it—implement it.

1. Write down your specific goal with metrics and a deadline

2. Identify your 3-5 progressive milestones

3. List the 3 most critical daily actions that will drive progress

4. Design a simple tracking method (digital or physical)

5. Schedule your first weekly review session

This isn't just another chapter to passively consume—it's the moment where your mental mastery transforms into real-world results.

This systematic approach dramatically shifts the traditional "success equation." Most people spend 90% of their efforts on tactics and only 10% on mental preparation. This book inverts that approach: when you master what happens above the shoulders—as we've systematically done through resilience, mental forging, mindset control, narrative rewriting, and thought pattern debugging—the execution becomes almost automatic.

Negative thought loops are like running on a mental treadmill—burning energy without gaining ground. The goal achievement system you've built is the opposite. It's like programming a GPS for your mind, making sure every step moves you measurably closer to your destination.

As we move into the next chapter, remember this fundamental truth: what happens above the shoulders—how you structure your thinking, focus your mind, and design your systems—determines what happens below them. The architecture of achievement is first built in our minds before a single brick is laid in the physical world.

Next, we'll take this achievement system to an even higher level by exploring "How Champions Are Made." You've built the mental framework for goal achievement—now you'll discover how elite performers maintain their edge when the stakes rise and the pressure intensifies. The mental systems that separate true champions from those who merely show promise aren't complicated—but they are profound, and they'll transform how you approach every meaningful challenge in your life.

Are you ready to transform how you pursue goals by mastering the science of mental focus? The system is here. The knowledge is in your hands. Now comes the moment of decision—will this be one more interesting idea you read about, or the turning point where everything changes?

CHAPTER 7: THE CHAMPION MINDSET—HOW CHAMPIONS ARE MADE

The champion mindset isn't something you're born with—it's built systematically through the mental mastery principles we've explored throughout this book. To truly understand what happens when resilience, mental forging, mindset control, narrative mastery, negative thought debugging, and goal achievement systems integrate perfectly, we need to see them embodied in real champions. Their stories reveal how the "90% above the shoulders" philosophy manifests when applied with extraordinary discipline.

Two Paths to Mastery

In this chapter, we'll explore two radically different approaches to mental mastery through the stories of Olympic medalists who built champion mindsets from entirely different starting points:

The Artist: Alex Ferreira transformed from "the worst kid on the mountain" to 2X Olympic medalist through emotional resilience, visualization, and falling in love with the process.

The Engineer: Alex Kopacz applied analytical precision to turn a casual 60-meter dash into Olympic gold in bobsleigh in just five years, breaking down seemingly impossible challenges into solvable variables.

These contrasting journeys prove that mental mastery isn't a one-size-fits-all formula but a set of adaptable principles that work regardless of your natural tendencies, background, or chosen field. You'll discover which approach resonates most with your own thinking style—and how to apply their battle-tested methods to your own impossible goal.

The Artist's Journey: Alex Ferreira and The Moment of Truth

The air at the top of the halfpipe was so cold it burned Alex Ferreira's lungs with each breath. Thousands of spectators had fallen silent at the 2024 Winter X Games, their collective gaze locked on the lone figure standing at the edge of destiny. The scoreboard told a brutal story: two falls, zero points, one final chance.

Most would have crumbled under the weight of that moment. Years of training, countless sacrifices, all the visualization sessions—all of it hanging by a thread.

Alex closed his eyes.

In the space of three deep breaths, something remarkable happened inside his mind. The roar of the crowd faded. The sting of his previous falls vanished. The crushing pressure transformed into pure, focused energy.

This is what champions do differently. While others panic, they find clarity. While others doubt, they decide.

With ice-cold composure, Alex dropped in.

The next 30 seconds weren't just a ski run—they were living proof that what happens above the shoulders determines everything below them. His body twisted through the air with impossible precision—each trick flowing seamlessly into the next, a physical manifestation of perfect mental harmony. When he landed his final move—a gravity-defying double cork 1620—the judges scrambled to comprehend what they had just witnessed.

The scoreboard flashed. The crowd erupted. Redemption.

To the casual observer, it looked like raw talent—another gifted athlete doing what gifted athletes do.

But I knew better. I knew the real story of a kid whose greatest talent wasn't skiing—it was the relentless training of his mind.

The Connection

I first met Alex back in 2017 during a video and photo shoot we were doing. What struck me wasn't his athletic credentials—it was the intensity with which he listened. While other athletes worked the room, Alex leaned in when people spoke, asking thoughtful questions, genuinely connecting. It's the same focus he brings to his craft.

Over the years, I've had the privilege of watching his journey unfold —not just as an observer, but as someone lucky enough to call him a friend. Alex isn't just an example I'm using to make a point. He's someone who embodies everything I've been telling you about the power of mindset.

A friend of mine once told me a story about Alex after a major competition in Europe. While other athletes rushed to media interviews and sponsor events, Alex stayed behind, helping young skiers adjust their form, offering quiet encouragement. No cameras. No recognition. Just genuine dedication to his craft.

"Couldn't that wait until tomorrow?" my friend had asked him.

"Tomorrow he might have given up," Alex replied simply. "The moment someone decides they can't do something is the moment they're right."

That's when I understood: Alex doesn't just ski from above the shoulders—he lives from above the shoulders. Every choice, every interaction, every setback is filtered through the same mental framework that turned him from an underdog into a champion.

They say you become the average of the five people you spend the most time with. If that's true, I'd consider myself fortunate to absorb even a fraction of Alex's mental toughness—his unwavering belief that what happens in your mind creates what happens in your life.

His story demolishes the comfortable excuse so many of us hide behind: that success belongs to the naturally gifted. What you're about to learn will transform how you view your own potential.

"I Was the Worst Kid on the Mountain"

Boston, midnight. Steam rose from sewer grates as Alex and I walked through the city after an event, streetlights casting long shadows on wet pavement. The temperature had dropped below freezing, but neither of us noticed—we were deep in conversation.

"How did it feel," I asked him, "when you realized you had what it takes to be world-class?"

Alex's laugh cut through the cold air, creating a small cloud in front of his face. "You're assuming I was always good at this." He stopped walking and turned to me. "Truth? I was the worst kid in my ski club. Not middle of the pack—dead last."

I was stunned. The Olympic medalist standing before me—the man whose posters hang on aspiring skiers' walls—started at the absolute bottom?

"Growing up in Aspen," he continued as we walked, "I was surrounded by kids who were naturals. They'd float above the half-pipe like they were born there." He shook his head, remembering. "Meanwhile, I'm face-planting every third attempt. My gear was handed down, my technique was awful. I was the kid coaches looked past."

The vulnerability in his voice struck me. Most of us hide our beginnings, especially when they're humble. But Alex owned his.

"Most Saturdays," he said, "I'd watch these other kids getting picked for special training groups while I was still trying to figure out how not to crash. Do you know how that feels? To want something so badly while every bit of evidence tells you that you don't have what it takes?"

I do know. And I bet you do too. We've all stood at the bottom of a mountain—literal or metaphorical—looking up at others who seem to ascend effortlessly while we struggle with the first step.

"So what made you different?" I asked. "Why didn't you quit?"

Alex stopped at a small coffee shop, still open despite the late hour. After ordering, he warmed his hands around the cup and answered.

"Two things. First, I couldn't imagine my life without skiing. It wasn't just something I did—it was part of who I was, even when I sucked at it." He took a sip. "Second, I had this crazy idea that if I worked twice as hard as the naturals, eventually I'd catch up. Then three times as hard to get ahead."

The turning point came unexpectedly. After months of failed attempts at a 360—a basic trick by professional standards—he finally landed one. Barely.

"It was the ugliest 360 you've ever seen," he laughed. "Wobbly, off-axis, I nearly lost it on the landing. But something clicked in my brain when my skis touched down. That single moment of success after hundreds of failures—it was like the universe whispering, 'See? It's possible.'"

That wobbly 360 wasn't just a physical breakthrough. It was cognitive evidence that rewired his belief system. It proved that what happens above the shoulders—persistence, belief, mental resilience—could overcome physical limitations and natural disadvantages.

"After that day," Alex said, his eyes reflecting the city lights, "I never again looked at the talented kids and thought, 'I can't compete with that.' Instead, I thought, 'I just need more time, more reps, more mental toughness.'"

That shift in perspective—from "I can't" to "Not yet"—exemplifies the growth mindset we explored in Chapter 3. His focus on effort over innate talent—"if I worked twice as hard as the naturals, eventually I'd catch up"—demonstrates exactly how the "YET Power" transforms perceived limitations into temporary challenges. This mental shift became the invisible dividing line between those who reach their potential and those who abandon it.

Built by the Grind

Behind every overnight success is usually a decade of invisible work. Alex's story is no exception.

His parents embodied the work ethic he would eventually become legendary for. His father, an Argentinian immigrant, waited tables at an upscale Aspen restaurant, often working until 2 AM. His mother worked as an esthetician, spending long hours on her feet taking care of clients while still raising a family. Together, they scraped by to keep their household afloat in one of America's most expensive zip codes.

"They'd do anything to keep me skiing," Alex told me, his voice softening with gratitude. "I watched them push through exhaustion day after day, year after year. How could I possibly complain about being tired? How could I not give everything when they were sacrificing so much?"

This wasn't just about skiing anymore. It was about honoring their sacrifice with his effort.

While natural talent took a vacation, discipline showed up every single day. Alex's routine would make most adults flinch:

MORNING

5:35 AM: Wake up – While others sleep, champions rise

6:00 AM: Mental preparation – Meditation, film study, and visualization

7:30 AM: Physical foundation – Gym training and decision training (trading)

9:15 AM: Sport-specific practice – Simulating aerial tricks and body awareness training

MIDDAY

11:00 AM: Recovery and reinforcement – Cold/hot contrast therapy with mental affirmations

1:00 PM: Creative work – Content creation and performance analysis

AFTERNOON/EVENING

3:00 PM: Skill expansion – Reading and learning new capabilities beyond skiing

5:00 PM: Business development – Building his brand and legacy beyond athletics (@HotdogHans)

8:00 PM: Sleep – Recovery is where growth happens

. . .

"Most people think skiing is all instinct and feel," Alex explained as we hiked a trail in Snowmass the following summer. "But there's this whole scientific side that separates the elite from everyone else."

He pulled out his phone and showed me an app filled with technical notes, frame-by-frame video analyses, and precise measurements of angles and rotations.

"I'd film every run, then break it down like game film," he said. "I noticed that if I adjusted my left shoulder position by just two inches on takeoff, I could add 15 degrees more rotation with the same effort. Little tweaks like that compound over time."

This obsessive attention to detail wasn't just physical fine-tuning—it was mental programming. Each repetition wasn't just building muscle memory; it was carving neural pathways that would activate under pressure. The science is clear: physical practice combined with mental visualization creates stronger neural connections than physical practice alone.

One technique Alex religiously practiced: Before bed each night, he would mentally replay his best run of the day three times in perfect detail, then visualize making it even better. This primed his subconscious to work on solutions while he slept—a phenomenon neuroscientists call "offline processing."

"The craziest thing would happen," he told me. "I'd struggle with a trick all day, then go to sleep thinking about it. The next morning, something would click. My body somehow knew the adjustment needed. It's like my brain kept working while I was sleeping."

During visualization, Alex didn't just see himself performing—he felt it. The g-forces during turns. The compression on landing. The specific tension in his core during rotations. This multisensory mental practice activated the same neural networks that fire during actual performance, creating a mental blueprint that his body could follow under pressure.

Alex's visualization practice takes the Mental Movie Method to Olympic levels. While most people visualize vague success, Alex goes all in—applying multisensory immersion with total precision. He feels every sensation, hears every sound, and sees every cue exactly as it unfolds. That level of detailed rehearsal carved neural highways in his brain—giving him a competitive advantage when the pressure was highest.

I had to work twice as hard to be half as good at first," he said with characteristic humility. "But here's what most people miss—if you keep doubling your effort while others plateau, eventually you don't just catch up. You blow right past them."

That relentless grind—years of methodical, intelligent work while nobody was watching—built a foundation so solid that by the time talent scouts finally noticed him, it was already too late for his competitors. The gap wasn't closing; it was widening with each passing season.

The Dinner Before the Breakthrough

February 2018. Mammoth, California. The final night of the competition where athletes would be named to the Olympic team.

I had organized a dinner with several of our athletes, sports agents, and industry insiders. The restaurant hummed with animated conversation about the upcoming Olympics in PyeongChang, South Korea—now just weeks away.

And there, in the middle of it all, sat Alex—quietly studying a video on his phone.

I slid into the seat next to him. "Last-minute cramming?"

He glanced up, offering a smile that didn't reach his eyes. Something was troubling him.

"Everything okay?" I asked.

He hesitated, then showed me his phone. It was a side-by-side comparison of his run and that of his chief competitor. The differences were nearly imperceptible to my untrained eye.

"See that?" he pointed to a slight variation in hand position during a specific trick. "That's costing me height on the back end. If I don't fix it..."

His voice trailed off. The weight of the moment suddenly felt very real. In a few short weeks, he would drop into the Olympic halfpipe with millions watching. Years of work distilled into three runs.

The server approached, offering drinks. The other athletes ordered beers and cocktails—a traditional toast to making the team.

"Just water for me," Alex said quietly.

When the server left, I nudged him. "You old enough to drink?"

He laughed—the tension momentarily broken. "Yeah, but that's not going to get me any closer to my goal."

It wasn't said as a boast. It wasn't said for effect. It was a simple statement of purpose—the quiet certainty of someone who had mentally rehearsed success so many times that any other outcome seemed inconceivable.

When the Olympics arrived, as the world watched, Alex charged the halfpipe with such precision and confidence that he earned an Olympic silver medal. He wasn't an alternate or a fill-in. He was exactly where he had trained his mind to believe he would be—on the podium.

He would go on to medal again in the following Olympics, throwing combinations that left the announcers struggling for words and competitors exchanging glances of disbelief.

"I'd study the best guys obsessively," he told me once. "Tanner Hall, Johnny Moseley—guys I once thought were from another planet. I'd fall a million times trying to match them, then push it a little further. Their success wasn't intimidating—it was informative."

That's the Alex Ferreira formula, the mental approach that defines true champions: outwork everyone behind the scenes, outlast the doubt during the low points, and when the world finally pays attention? Leave them wondering how you made the impossible look inevitable.

Beyond the Medals—The Soul of a Skier

January 2023. Aspen, Colorado. The sun cast long shadows across Buttermilk Mountain as the day's final light painted the snow in amber hues. Most skiers had packed up hours ago, but one lone figure remained—a silhouette against the darkening sky, still training like the Crystal Globe was on the line.

I watched Alex from the base of the halfpipe, marveling not at his technical perfection, but at the pure joy evident in every movement. After two Olympic medals, three X Games golds, and World Cup victories, he still approached each run with the enthusiasm of that kid who once celebrated landing his first wobbly 360.

Later, as we sat on a wooden bench watching the alpenglow illuminate the peaks, I asked him the question that had been on my mind:

"After achieving everything you've dreamed of... why do you still push so hard?"

Alex was quiet for a moment, his breath visible in the cold mountain air.

"You know what's crazy?" he finally said. "Most people think reaching the top would feel like arriving somewhere. Like once you get there, you're done." He shook his head. "But that's not how it works at all."

He pointed toward the halfpipe, now cast in shadow.

"Every day I drop in, I discover something new—some tiny adjustment, some feeling, some connection I never noticed before. The medals are cool, but they're not why I'm still here. I'm here because I'm still in love with the discovery."

That year, Alex collaborated with a drone cinematographer to capture what that love looks like in motion. The resulting footage—Alex carving through Aspen's backcountry with a camera chasing his every move—went viral not because of technical perfection, but because it showed what it means to achieve mastery without losing the pure joy that fueled the beginning of the journey.

"Watch a little kid learn to ski," Alex said. "They fall, they laugh, they get up and try again. No ego, no expectations—just pure exploration. The secret to staying at the top isn't just working harder than everyone else. It's keeping that childlike curiosity alive even when you're at the pinnacle."

This focus extends beyond his personal performance. One afternoon, I watched him work with a frustrated teenager who kept crashing on a basic trick. After an hour of patient coaching, the kid finally nailed it. The look on his face—pure electric joy—was mirrored perfectly on Alex's.

"If I can help one kid land their first trick and feel that fire inside," he told me later, "that's worth more than any medal. Because I know exactly what that moment can do—how it can change everything above the shoulders. How it can rewrite what you believe is possible."

The Engineer's Approach: Alex Kopacz and Systematic Success

While Alex Ferreira's journey shows us the power of persistence and process-driven excellence, there's more than one path to developing a champion's mindset. What happens when we apply the "above the shoulders" principle to someone with an entirely different background and approach?

Enter Alex Kopacz—a man who would rewrite the rules of what's possible when you combine raw analytical thinking with unwavering mental discipline.

The Engineer Who Redesigned Athletic Success

"I don't see problems—I see variables that need to be isolated and solved."

This wasn't a scientist speaking about a laboratory experiment. This was Alex Kopacz—Olympic bobsledder—explaining how he approached a sport that sends athletes hurtling down an ice track at 150 kilometers per hour.

The Canadian bobsleigh community didn't welcome Kopacz with open arms when he first appeared. Far from it.

"People weren't exactly rolling out the red carpet," Kopacz told me when we first sat down to discuss his journey. We connected instantly at an event with other athletes, forming a brotherhood that continues today. "I was an outsider, a newcomer—and my size, strength, and speed made a lot of established athletes feel threatened."

At 6'5" and nearly 280 pounds of explosive power, Kopacz had the kind of physique that turned heads. But it wasn't his appearance that would ultimately define him—it was what lived above his shoulders.

Kopacz's path to Olympic glory wasn't the carefully plotted trajectory most elite athletes follow. While most Olympic champions begin training in their sport as children, Kopacz was 23 years old and finishing his mechanical engineering degree when fate intervened during a university track meet.

"I was a shot putter," Alex explained, "just training for varsity competition. During one practice, I decided to run a 60-meter dash. I clocked 7.24 seconds—fast enough that someone suggested I try out for bobsleigh."

Think about that for a moment. Most people at 23 have already decided who they are and what they're capable of. Their mindset is fixed: "This is my path. These are my limits." But Alex possessed something far more valuable than raw athletic talent—he had a mindset that remained open to possibility.

The Mental Edge: When Talent Isn't Enough

What makes Alex's story so compelling isn't just that he switched sports late—it's that he entered a world where everyone else had years of specialized experience. In the face of that disadvantage, most people would have thought: "I'm too far behind. I'll never catch up." Alex thought differently.

"I knew I was starting from zero," he said. "But instead of seeing that as a disadvantage, I saw it as freedom. I had no bad habits to unlearn. I could build my technique from scratch."

This mindset—this refusal to let circumstances dictate possibility—is what separates champions from everyone else. While his competitors relied on experience, Alex leveraged his mental approach.

His first tests came early and ruthlessly. During his initial runs as a bobsleigh novice, Kopacz experienced multiple crashes that would have sent most people back to safer pursuits.

"I felt completely disoriented and terrified," he told me. "Imagine being trapped in a washing machine going 150 kilometers per hour down an ice track. Your body is getting slammed in every direction while your mind is screaming to make it stop."

Yet after each crash, he forced himself back onto the track. When I asked him how, he revealed the mental framework that would define his career:

"My engineering brain took over. I broke down the problem, isolated variables, and approached it methodically. Where others saw crashes, I saw data points. Each failure taught me something specific about weight distribution, entry angles, or muscle tension. The fear was still there, but my analytical process gave me a way to work through it."

This engineering mindset became his secret weapon. "Most athletes rely on instinct or what 'feels right,'" he explained. "I approached bobsleigh as a physics problem to be solved. When you're converting raw power into sled acceleration, every motion can be optimized if you have the right mental model."

Kopacz's systematic breakdown of bobsleigh physics applied the same *Bite-Sized Wins* strategy we explored in Chapter 1. Just as I focused on "three more steps" when that desert dune seemed insurmountable, Kopacz transformed the overwhelming challenge of mastering a new sport into analyzable components, making the impossible manageable through mental strategy.

But resilience isn't just about mental approach—it's about physical perseverance too. After finishing a development circuit on the North American tracks, Alex's next year took him to the World Cup team. His first World Champs experience was made memorable by contracting pneumonia—an ordeal that would sideline most athletes

"My lungs were compromised. Breathing was difficult. Every push felt like my chest was on fire," Kopacz recalled. "But I kept thinking: The pain is temporary. The regret of giving up is permanent."

While Alex Ferreira channeled his mental energy through visualization and emotional resilience, Kopacz approached challenges with systematic problem-solving. Two different mindsets, yet both leading to the same outcome: overcoming what seemed impossible.

Gritting through the illness, he helped push his team to an eighth-place finish at the 2015 World Championships. This wasn't just athletic performance—it was mental mastery in action.

Kopacz discovered what so many of us fail to realize: the barrier between impossible and achievable exists primarily in our minds. While his body struggled with pneumonia, his mindset refused to acknowledge any outcome except pushing forward.

"There's this moment in every major challenge," Kopacz told me, "where your body is screaming to stop but your mind has to make a choice. Most people listen to the screaming. Champions learn to hear it as just background noise."

The Ultimate Sacrifice

Alex quickly realized that if he wanted to become truly world-class, he needed world-class coaching. The problem? The only coach who could take him to the next level lived in Germany.

"That meant leaving everything behind—family, friends, the comfort of home—to train in a country where I barely spoke the language and knew almost no one," Alex said.

Most people would have balked at this sacrifice. The comfort of the familiar is powerfully seductive. But Alex understood something crucial about mental toughness: growth happens outside your comfort zone.

In Germany, Alex trained under two-time Olympic champion Olaf Hampel, embracing a level of discipline that bordered on obsession. Every detail mattered: sprint mechanics, strength development, mental conditioning, ice-track technique.

"There were so many nights I questioned everything," Alex admitted. "Missing birthdays back home, holidays, feeling isolated. But I kept my focus on one clear goal: I wanted to be so good they couldn't possibly leave me off the Olympic team."

This unwavering commitment—this ability to sacrifice immediate comfort for long-term greatness—is perhaps the most important mental quality a champion can possess. Most people quit when the path becomes difficult. Champions understand that difficulty is the path.

The Olympic Moment: Where Preparation Meets Opportunity

Just weeks later, in February 2018, just five years after first sitting in a bobsleigh, Kopacz's mental fortitude culminated at the Winter Olympics in PyeongChang, South Korea. Partnered with his pilot in the two-man bobsleigh, they entered the final day of competition just 0.10 seconds behind the leaders.

The night before their final runs, Kopacz barely slept. "Everything we'd worked for came down to these moments," he recalled. "But rather than letting the pressure crush me, I channeled it. I visualized myself as a human rocket at the start—completely focused on transferring maximum energy into the sled."

Before that final run, his coach simply told him, "Just do what we've done a thousand times." This simple reminder—to trust their preparation—was all Kopacz needed to hear.

He described those final moments at the starting line: "It was our race to lose. We were the leaders going into that final run, and being last off, you become very aware of that fact that mistakes are no longer an option. My heart pounded so hard I could feel my racing suit vibrating. The cold bit into my face, but my hands felt hot in my thin gloves. The crowd noise faded into a distant hum. I tasted metal—adrenaline's signature. All I heard was my breathing and the countdown beeps. Then, as we exploded from the start, everything disappeared except the sled and the ice."

As their sled rocketed down the icy track on their final run, every turn, every subtle shift of weight, represented years of sacrifice. When they crossed the finish line, the clock showed they were 0.01 seconds ahead—they thought they'd won outright.

Then came confusion. The scoreboard showed something unprecedented: a time of 3:16.86—identical to the German team's time.

For just the second time in Olympic history, the gold medal would be shared.

"The moment was surreal," Kopacz told me. "When we realized we had tied, there was this beautiful moment of mutual respect. Both teams celebrated together on the podium. I couldn't have written a better ending."

He added, "Standing there, medal around my neck, feeling its weight—solid and real against my chest—I wasn't thinking about the physical journey. I was thinking about the mental one—all the moments I could have quit but chose to continue, all the times I chose discomfort over ease because I knew what waited on the other side."

The gold medal validated his approach—his willingness to apply an engineer's precision to an athlete's passion had created something remarkable. Kopacz had proven that the mental framework you bring to a challenge matters more than the challenge itself.

"People often ask if I was surprised to win gold," he reflected. "The truth is, I would have been more surprised if we hadn't. Not because I'm arrogant, but because I'd meticulously engineered every variable in my control for that outcome. The mind decides first what the body will achieve later. Olympic champions aren't made on race day—they're made in the thousands of moments when no one is watching but choices are being made."

Beyond Athletic Achievement: Finding Purpose Through Service

While many athletes struggle with the vacuum that follows Olympic success, Kopacz's mindset allowed him to pivot toward new forms of fulfillment. The gold medal, he discovered, wasn't the destination but merely a milestone in his ongoing growth.

"After winning gold, I realized the medal wasn't the end goal—it was just proof that the process worked," he told me during one of our conversations. "The real reward was who I became along the way."

This realization led Kopacz to explore how his mindset could create value beyond the competitive arena. During a service trip we took together to Thailand, we found ourselves building a frog farm for a local community under the blazing sun.

The humid air clung to our skin like a hot towel. Sweat carved rivulets through the dirt on our faces and arms as we dug through clay-heavy soil. The project wasn't glamorous—nothing like standing on an Olympic podium—yet I noticed something remarkable in Kopacz's demeanor. Despite the heat and discomfort, he was more energized than I'd ever seen him.

Sweat dripping down his face, Kopacz turned to me with unexpected sincerity. "You know what I love about this?" he said. "For years as an athlete, everything was about me—my training, my performance, my goals. It felt selfish. Now, helping others gives me something the gold medal couldn't."

This revelation struck me deeply. Here was an Olympic champion finding more satisfaction in serving others than in standing on the podium. This wasn't just resilience—it was growth.

The Ultimate Test: When Mindset Faces Mortality

If Olympic competition tests an athlete's mental fortitude, what Kopacz faced next would require a level of psychological resilience few of us can imagine. Three years after his Olympic victory, at age 31, he was hospitalized with a severe, life-threatening illness, his powerful athlete's body suddenly betraying him.

The stakes had changed dramatically. No longer competing for medals, he was fighting for his life.

"I was on oxygen, my condition deteriorating so rapidly that I drafted a will and said goodbye to my family," Kopacz recalled, his voice quiet. He called me during this time.

We talked for a good while that night—sharing tears, recalling special moments, and reminiscing about fun memories. When I finally hung up the phone, I told my wife about our conversation and that it could be the last one I'd ever have with him. It was a restless night and one I'll never forget.

Picture the scene: The antiseptic smell of the hospital room. The rhythmic beeping of monitors. The rasp of oxygen flowing through tubes. The crushing weight on his chest with each labored breath. These sensations defined his world as doctors discussed increasingly dire scenarios outside his door.

This wasn't a starting line with Olympic glory waiting at the finish. This was a battle where victory simply meant surviving another day.

Yet even here, facing his own mortality, the champion's mindset prevailed. He approached recovery with the same methodical determination that earned him Olympic gold.

"What got me through wasn't physical strength—it was mental resilience built through years of athletic challenges," he explained. "I set tiny daily goals: first walking to the bathroom unassisted, then walking to the end of my driveway, progressively rebuilding."

This approach mirrored exactly how he had tackled bobsleigh years earlier—breaking down seemingly impossible challenges into measurable, achievable steps. The same mental framework that transformed him from novice to Olympic champion now guided his recovery from life-threatening illness.

Alex Kopacz's approach to recovery—*"first walking to the bathroom unassisted, then walking to the end of my driveway"*—was the same *Bite-Sized Wins* strategy that helped me conquer that unrelenting desert dune. Whether you're facing Olympic competition or fighting your way back from a hospital bed, breaking overwhelming challenges into manageable steps remains a cornerstone of mental mastery.

"When doctors told me recovery would be slow, I didn't hear 'impossible.' I heard 'complex problem that needs systematic solutions,'" Kopacz told me. "Just like in bobsleigh, I focused on controlling variables—nutrition, movement, rest, mental focus—and measuring incremental improvements."

This wasn't coincidence. The mindset Kopacz had cultivated for sport became the foundation for overcoming life's greatest challenges. His story illustrates that mental frameworks aren't sport-specific or career-specific—they're life tools that transfer across any domain.

"In that hospital bed, I remembered something crucial," he shared. "The body can only go as far as the mind allows it to. My body was failing, but my mind refused to accept defeat as an option."

"I built a home gym with a squat rack, started with long walks with my dog, listening to audiobooks on philosophy and leadership for mental clarity," he explained. "Every day, I focused not on how far I had to go, but on making that day's effort better than the last."

This approach—breaking seemingly impossible challenges into manageable daily improvements—is the essence of mental toughness. It's not about grand gestures; it's about consistent action toward a focused goal.

The Mindset Legacy

Today, Kopacz doesn't just tell his story—he lives it. He founded a medical device company, coaches Olympic hopefuls, and speaks to audiences about the power of mindset. While competing at the elite level, he even completed a physics degree in 2018, showing his commitment to intellectual growth alongside athletic excellence.

After winning his gold medal, Kopacz took it to visit his elementary school, letting every child hold it and telling them it was "their gold medal too" because community support had made his journey possible. This wasn't just a nice gesture—it reflected his understanding that success is never truly individual.

The mental approach that transformed Kopacz from university shot-putter to Olympic champion in just five years offers powerful lessons for anyone facing challenges that seem beyond their capabilities. Consider how these principles might apply to your own life:

REFRAME problems into puzzles.

Rather than being deterred by crashes or setbacks, he reframed them as data points in an ongoing experiment. "The biggest lesson I learned is that limitations are mostly self-imposed," he explained. "I had no business becoming an Olympic champion in five years, but I refused to accept that narrative." Ask yourself: What overwhelming challenge in your life could be broken down into smaller, solvable problems?

TRANSFORM suffering into teaching.

Through pneumonia, injury, and eventually life-threatening illness, he focused on what he could control rather than what he couldn't. His approach to recovery mirrored his athletic development—methodical, measured, and relentlessly forward-looking. Ask yourself: What difficult experience are you currently facing that might contain valuable lessons?

EMBRACE total ownership.

When the bobsleigh community didn't welcome him, he didn't blame others; he worked harder to prove his worth. "I think what separated me was my all-in mentality," he explained. "When I decided to pursue bobsleigh, I didn't just dip my toe in—I dove headfirst." Ask yourself: In what area of your life are you blaming circumstances instead of taking full responsibility?

CHOOSE long-term vision over short-term comfort.

Moving to Germany to train wasn't easy, but it was necessary for his ultimate goal. In his words: "Comfort and growth rarely coexist. I had to choose which one mattered more." Ask yourself: What immediate comfort are you prioritizing that's keeping you from your greater goal?

CULTIVATE perspective through gratitude.

Even at his lowest moments, Kopacz focused on appreciation rather than frustration. "People talk about the physical demands," he said, "but bobsleigh is 90% mental. You're hurling yourself down an ice track at 150 km/h with milliseconds to make decisions. The mind has to be stronger than the fear." Ask yourself: How might practicing gratitude change your perspective on your current challenges?

FIND fulfillment through serving others.

After achieving the highest athletic honor, he discovered that helping others brought even greater satisfaction than personal achievement. "Gold medals tarnish," he told me, "but the impact you have on others endures." Ask yourself: How could your skills and experiences be used to make a meaningful difference for someone else?

MEASURE progress systematically.

From bobsleigh training to his near-death experience, Kopacz tracked specific metrics to validate his approach and maintain motivation. "What gets measured improves," he explained. "When you collect data on your progress, setbacks become information, not failure." Ask yourself: What key indicators could you track to make your progress more visible and your approach more scientific?

These principles aren't just interesting reflections—they're a blueprint for approaching any challenge, whether in sports, business, relationships, or personal growth. The frameworks that guided Kopacz from engineering student to Olympic champion to recovery from life-threatening illness are universally applicable.

In our final conversation about his journey, Kopacz offered a perspective that perfectly encapsulates the central message of this book:

"If I've learned anything, it's that life truly is 90% above the shoulders. My physical capabilities didn't change dramatically from day one to Olympic gold—what transformed was my mental approach. I engineered a mindset that refused to recognize conventional limitations, that treated obstacles as data points rather than stop signs, and that systematically solved for success rather than accepting failure. The gold medal is nice, but the real victory was mastering what happens between my ears."

He paused, then added something I'll never forget: "Most people spend their lives at the mercy of their thoughts. Champions learn to put their thoughts at the mercy of their vision."

PAUSE HERE: This is your moment to transform theory into practice. Take Kopacz's methodical approach—his ability to break seemingly impossible challenges into manageable steps—and apply it directly to that goal you've been carrying since the beginning of this book.

What are the first three micro-steps that would dissolve the intimidation factor of your larger ambition? Just as Kopacz converted "recovery from life-threatening illness" into "walking to the bathroom unassisted," what equivalent stepping stones would make your path forward clear and actionable?

Jot these steps down now. This simple act of translation—from concept to concrete action—is where your brain begins to literally rewire itself, creating new neural pathways that transform obstacles into opportunities.

This isn't abstract theory—this is where transformation happens. By defining your next three manageable steps right now, you're literally rewiring your brain to see possibilities where you previously saw only obstacles.

The Champion's Blueprint: Five Universal Principles

As we've seen through the stories of Alex Ferreira and Alex Kopacz, the champion's mindset transcends sport, background, and circumstance. Though they pursued excellence in radically different disciplines—one soaring through the air on skis, the other hurtling down ice in a metal sled—the mental frameworks that propelled them to Olympic glory share striking similarities.

What makes these parallel stories so powerful is how differently these champions approach mental mastery. Ferreira relies on emotional resilience, visualization, and joy; Kopacz on analytical thinking, systematic problem-solving, and engineering principles. Their contrasting paths demonstrate that mental mastery isn't a one-size-fits-all formula but a set of adaptable principles that work regardless of your natural tendencies, background, or chosen field.

What can we learn from these two champions that applies universally? Here are the five foundational mindset principles that emerge when we analyze their journeys—five truths that embody the "above the shoulders" philosophy:

1. Mental Resilience Trumps Natural Talent Every Time

Both athletes faced significant disadvantages—Ferreira was "the worst kid on the mountain," while Kopacz entered a specialized sport a decade later than most competitors. Yet both achieved the pinnacle of success because they understood that psychological endurance matters more than genetic potential. They rewrote the narrative that success belongs only to the naturally gifted.

2. Visualization Is Precision Neural Programming, Not Just Positive Thinking

Both athletes used sophisticated mental rehearsal techniques to prepare their minds and bodies for peak performance. They didn't just imagine general success; they visualized specific sensations, movements, and scenarios with such detail that their nervous systems responded as if they were already experiencing it. This practice created neural pathways that activated under pressure.

3. Champions Fall in Love with the Process, Not Just the Outcome

Both Ferreira and Kopacz found joy in the daily pursuit of excellence, not just in the medals they eventually won. While others celebrated victories, they were already analyzing improvements for the next challenge. This obsession with continuous growth prevented them from being satisfied with "good enough" and pushed them to explore the outer limits of their potential.

4. Setbacks Are Transformed into Data, Not Defeat

When faced with crashes, injuries, illness, or failure, both athletes responded with problem-solving rather than emotional drama. They systematically extracted lessons from every setback, converting apparent obstacles into stepping stones for growth. This analytical approach to adversity allowed them to bounce back stronger after experiences that would have broken less resilient minds.

5. Champions Embrace Total Ownership of Their Journey

Neither athlete blamed external circumstances for their struggles. When faced with disadvantages—whether it was starting behind, facing rejection, or dealing with illness—they focused exclusively on what they could control. This ownership mindset eliminated excuses and channeled all available energy toward productive action.

These Olympic champions don't just demonstrate isolated mental techniques—they embody the complete *Mental Mastery Pyramid* we've built throughout this book:

Foundation: Resilience — Both athletes demonstrate extraordinary persistence through setbacks

Structure: Mental Forge — Both continuously strengthen their minds through deliberate challenge

Operating System: Mindset Control — Both maintain precise control over their thoughts and focus

Programming: Narrative Mastery — Both rewrite their identity stories to support their growth

Debugging: Thought Pattern Correction — Both instantly recognize and redirect negative spirals

Application: Goal Achievement — Both implement systematic approaches to performance

Integration: Champion Mindset — Both combine all these elements into a unified mental approach

Your Champion's Path: From Inspiration to Implementation

These stories light up a clear path for your own impossible goal—the one that seemed so far out of reach when you started this book. It doesn't matter if you're wired more like Ferreira (visualization and emotional resilience) or Kopacz (analytical and methodical). The mental game plan works either way.

In a world obsessed with finding shortcuts to success, these two champions stand as living proof of this book's central message: Life truly is 90% above the shoulders. The question isn't whether you have what it takes to achieve excellence in your field. After reading these stories, it's clear that the real question is: Are you willing to train your mind with the same dedication that these champions trained theirs?

As we move into the next Chapter, we'll build on this champion's mindset to explore how to hardwire "never quit" into your neural pathways, ensuring that your mental mastery becomes not just a skill set but a fundamental part of who you are—your DNA. You'll learn how top performers across disciplines push past their *Breakthrough Threshold*—that critical point where most people stop but champions continue—to consistently shatter performance barriers.

But first, take a moment to reflect on which aspect of the champion's mindset—Ferreira's emotional resilience and visualization or Kopacz's analytical approach—resonates more strongly with your natural tendencies. There's no right answer. The beauty of mental mastery is that it can be approached from multiple directions while achieving the same transformative results.

Implementation Challenge:

This week, identify one specific technique from either Alex Ferreira or Alex Kopacz that you'll implement daily. Whether it's Ferreira's multisensory visualization practice or Kopacz's systematic data collection approach, commit to applying it consistently for seven days. Document your experience, noting any shifts in your performance, problem-solving ability, or emotional state. Remember, champions aren't born—they're built, one mental practice at a time.

This isn't just another exercise—it's your next critical step toward that impossible goal. By implementing these champion-level mental techniques consistently, you're literally constructing the neural architecture required to transform what once seemed impossible into your inevitable reality. The gap between where you are and where you want to be exists primarily above your shoulders—and you've just been given the blueprint to bridge it.

CHAPTER 8: BUILDING 'NEVER QUIT' INTO YOUR DNA

The Genesis of Mental Mastery

My lungs were on fire. Twelve hours into the Ironman, every muscle screamed for surrender. The Tennessee afternoon sun beat down mercilessly as I rounded the final corner of the marathon—the last grueling leg of my journey. My legs felt like concrete pillars, each step a negotiation between a body desperate to stop and a mind that refused to listen.

The world had narrowed to the strip of pavement directly in front of me. Each breath burned. Salt crystals formed white patterns on my skin. My heartbeat pounded in my ears like a tribal drum, drowning out everything but a single thought:

One more step. Just one more step.

"This is what it means to be truly alive," I realized, as spectators began to materialize along the route. "This is what it means to push beyond what everyone—including yourself—thought possible."

As the finish line came into view, something shifted—energy surged through my depleted body. Every dark, quiet morning, every mile, every moment of doubt had led me here. The months of sacrifice weren't just about training my body; they were about proving something to myself. And in that last stretch, the lesson was clear: mindset is everything. The body follows where the mind leads.

Long before I faced the brutal desert dunes of the Spartan race, this Ironman journey was forging the mental framework that would carry me through every challenge that followed. What appeared as practiced resilience during that desert race had its painful birth years earlier on these Tennessee roads and the steep climbs of Utah's Little Cottonwood Canyon.

"Ironman isn't just an event—it's a mindset that, once developed, becomes the foundation for everything else in your life." —Mark Allen, six-time Ironman World Champion

The Power of Six Words: Where Mental Mastery Begins

We all have that one friend who doubts us. The one who says things they don't think twice about but that stick with us forever.

"You definitely couldn't do it."

My coworker was training for triathlons and planned to work up to a full Ironman over several years. When I asked why he didn't just go all in, his dismissal came without hesitation. Six simple words, casually tossed aside like an afterthought.

But the moment I heard them, something shifted in my mind—that familiar sensation I'd later experience in wrestling matches when I recognized the exact moment my opponent mentally broke. This time, though, I wasn't facing another athlete. I was facing the most formidable opponent of all: doubt itself.

That's the thing about challenges—they reveal who you really are. When someone tells you that you can't do something, you have two choices: believe them or prove them wrong. The path you choose defines your life.

For those who don't know, an Ironman Triathlon is a 2.4-mile swim, followed by a 112-mile bike ride, and finished with a full 26.2-mile marathon—all back-to-back, all in one day. The swim tests your endurance and composure in open water. The bike ride demands sustained power and mental fortitude over hours of exertion. And the marathon? It pushes your body through exhaustion when every muscle screams to stop.

At the time, I had never done a triathlon of any kind. I could barely swim outside of a doggy paddle. I'd never run competitively in my life. I had a full-time job, a wife, and four kids.

Every logical part of my brain screamed, "This is ridiculous."

Instead, I signed up the next day.

Not because I was ready. Because I wanted to see if I could become the person who was.

Have you ever felt that spark of defiance when someone tells you what you can't do? That's the same fire that can forge you into someone stronger than you ever imagined. This spark—this transformation of doubt into determination—would later become the foundation of the resilience principles I shared in Chapter 1.

The Snowbird Challenge: The Laboratory of Mental Resilience

When I committed to the Ironman, I wasn't starting from zero when it came to mental toughness. Long before I took on the challenge of becoming an Ironman, I had been developing the mental endurance necessary for extreme challenges through another grueling test—one that had been shaping my mindset for years.

This mental training ground was the Snowbird Hill Climb, a 10-mile, 3,460-foot ascent in Utah's Little Cottonwood Canyon. While the Ironman would become my ultimate test of endurance, this canyon was where I first learned what it truly means to push beyond perceived limits and silence the voice that begs you to quit.

There's a moment in every crippling challenge when your body and mind conspire to break you. Your lungs sear, your legs turn to stone, and a voice inside begs you to stop. Most people surrender here. But if you can push past—one more pedal stroke, one more mile—you unearth a resilience you didn't know you possessed.

I learned this lesson over years chasing the Snowbird Hill Climb. This wasn't just a bike ride; it was a crucible that tested every limit I had.

Little Cottonwood Canyon isn't just a route—it's a monster. Carved by glaciers into a steep-walled trough, it climbs relentlessly from Salt Lake City's edge to Snowbird's base. To put it in perspective for non-cyclists, imagine walking up the steepest staircase you can find—then doing that for two straight hours without a break. The kind of climb where each turn reveals another punishing ascent, where the air thins as you gain elevation, and where your legs scream for mercy with every pedal stroke.

That canyon isn't just a road—it's alive. On gentler slopes, pine-scented breezes and the crunch of granite under tires seduce you. But hit those 10% grades and its true nature emerges—the asphalt rippling endlessly upward, mocking your burning quads and the metallic taste of effort coating your tongue.

I've ridden its 10 miles over 50 times—logged meticulously in data—and countless more unrecorded. Each ascent was a battle against grades that don't forgive weakness or self-doubt. If any place embodies who I am—my grit, my joy, my scars—it's this canyon.

The mind always quits before the body does. This isn't just a catchy phrase—it's scientific fact, and it would become the centerpiece of my mental mastery system.

The Breakthrough Threshold: The Brain's Greatest Lie

I wish someone had grabbed me by the shoulders years ago and told me this: Your brain is a liar.

Not about everything. Just about your limits.

Here's the truth I discovered the hard way, slogging up that mountain and stumbling through that Ironman: When your mind is screaming that you're completely tapped out—when every cell feels like it's shutting down and your internal voice is begging you to stop—you're nowhere near your actual capacity.

Let that sink in.

The moment you're convinced you've got nothing left is the moment you've still got a significant reserve in the tank. It's not just motivational garbage—it's neurological reality. Your brain has a built-in governor that slams the brakes long before you're in actual danger.

This principle—what I call the *Breakthrough Threshold*—is the cornerstone insight that would later inform every aspect of my approach to mental mastery. While resilience gives you the ability to persist, and deliberately facing challenges strengthens your cognitive capacity, the *Breakthrough Threshold* explains the neurological mechanism behind both.

Think of it as driving a Ferrari but never taking it out of second gear. Most people live their entire lives using only a fraction of their true capacity, never discovering the power that lies dormant under the hood.

Your brain is wired for survival, not optimization. It prioritizes energy conservation and self-preservation, which means it often signals fatigue or tells you to stop long before you actually need to. Scientists have a fancy name for this—they call it the Central Governor Theory —but what it really means is your brain acts like a speed limiter on a car engine, capping your performance before you hit a real limit. This understanding is revolutionizing approaches to everything from athletic training to treating chronic pain, where practitioners are finding that helping patients recognize their first threshold versus their actual capacity can dramatically improve outcomes.

Studies on perceived exertion show that when people think they're at 100%, they actually have significant energy reserves left untapped. When researchers led by Dr. Timothy Noakes, pioneer of the Central Governor Theory, applied electrical stimulation to muscles that subjects believed were completely exhausted, those same muscles could still produce substantial force—proving that physical failure begins in the mind.

The *Breakthrough Threshold* is the point where discomfort tells you to stop, but potential is still waiting on the other side. It's the invisible wall that separates ordinary effort from extraordinary results:

> The first threshold is your perceived limit (where most people stop)

> The second threshold is your actual limit (which is much further than you think)

> The gap between the two is where real breakthroughs happen

I've experienced this firsthand—even after years of training my mindset. During my early attempts at conquering that canyon, when the road reared up at 10%, my breathing labored, and my muscles screamed in protest, I'd believe the lie. I'd stop, rest, and vow to fight again another day.

But every great achievement in human history has come from someone who refused to believe that lie—someone who pushed beyond the first threshold into that breakthrough zone where transformation happens.

The Pool: Where Mental Resilience Is Born

My first day of Ironman training didn't just humble me—it shattered the illusion of who I thought I was.

I stood in front of the community pool in the early morning, towel draped over my shoulder. Most of the world was still asleep, and the pool was nearly empty. I carried the unearned confidence of someone who had never truly tested his limits. The reflection in the water stared back—a man who believed attitude alone could over-power reality. *"How hard could swimming really be?"* I thought. I'd spent my life in pools, roughhousing with my kids in the shallow end. If nothing else, I could dog-paddle.

The water was the first to tell me the truth.

The moment my body sliced through the surface, a cold reality rushed in with the chlorinated water. Twenty-five yards—that was my first objective. Just get to the other side of this community pool without stopping.

Halfway across, pure panic took hold. My brain short-circuited, sending chaotic messages to my limbs. My arms windmilled franti-cally, slapping at the water instead of pulling through it. Water flooded my nose and surged down my throat. My lungs burned as I gasped for air that wasn't there. The chemical smell of chlorine filled my sinuses as I fought against the growing sense that I was drowning in the shallow end of a community pool.

The rhythmic splashing, the muffled underwater silence between strokes, the chlorine vapor that seemed to penetrate every breath— the soundscape of the swim was as overwhelming as the physical challenge itself.

In the lanes on either side of me, the few early-morning swimmers glided with effortless rhythm, their casual workout a stark contrast to my desperate struggle to survive.

Twelve yards in, I surrendered. My feet found the pool bottom as I lurched upright, water streaming down my face, chest heaving violently, the taste of chlorine burning my throat. The sudden silence as I stopped thrashing hit me like judgment.

The few people there stared. Not just glanced—stared. The kind of looks you give a car wreck or a public meltdown. I'd failed to complete even a single length of a community pool.

"You okay?" asked a teenage lifeguard, clearly concerned.

I nodded, unable to form words between gasps, swallowing what little pride I had left.

That moment—standing breathless in the shallow end while others swam effortlessly past—was more than just embarrassment. It was a stark realization: in eight months, I was supposed to swim 2.4 miles in open water... and I couldn't even make it 25 yards in a controlled pool.

This was my first real Ironman test. It wasn't physical—it was in my head.

That raw, humbling experience didn't come with a framework or label. It just gave me one clear truth: *you keep going anyway.*

This is what separates the extraordinary from the average—the willingness to start at pathetic and work your way up to great.

Fifty-Plus Battles: The Laboratory of Mental Mastery

The sub-60-minute goal became my obsession, a years-long pursuit etched across over 50 logged rides and dozens more lost to memory.

Early attempts were punishing—90 to 120 minutes of suffering at slow speeds, the final 3 miles breaking me every single time. I'd hit the wall where the road reared up at its steepest, my brain screaming that it was impossible.

But each ride taught me something crucial about mental endurance: you don't conquer the mountain in one giant leap. You shrink it down —one turn, one pedal stroke at a time.

That instinct—to break the impossible into manageable chunks— would later become one of the most important strategies I ever developed. But back then, it wasn't a tool. It was survival.

Mental resilience isn't built through positive thinking—it's built through suffering and continuing anyway.

Mental endurance isn't built in comfortable moments of reflection— it's forged in the crucible of "Oh shit, I can't do this" followed by "But I'm going to anyway."

I developed specific mental strategies that carried me through the toughest sections:

Segmentation: I divided the climb into five sections, focusing only on completing the current segment rather than the entire mountain.

Mindful breathing: When my lungs burned, I counted breaths—four counts in, six counts out—creating a rhythm that calmed both body and mind.

Positive anchoring: I placed imaginary "anchors" at certain points on the climb—a distinctive tree, a particular bend— that triggered positive self-talk when I reached them.

The 'one more' technique: When I wanted to quit, I'd tell myself, "Just make it to the next switchback," then "just one more curve," repeatedly negotiating with myself until I reached the top.

You know this feeling. Maybe it's not a mountain you're climbing, but we all face moments when continuing seems impossible. The project deadline looming at midnight. The difficult conversation you're avoiding. The financial setback that seems insurmountable. In those moments, your mind is the battlefield where victory or defeat is determined.

My speeds gradually improved and my times dropped from 120 minutes to 90, then to 70. Each improvement wasn't just physical—it was rewiring my brain to push past the false limits my mind had set, to access the reserves I didn't know I had. This neurological rewiring process would later inform the mental forge concept I shared in Chapter 2, though at the time, I didn't have the framework to articulate what was happening in my brain.

The Triumph: Breaking Barriers

After years of suffering, victory came on a day that crystallized everything I'd learned about mental endurance in that canyon.

Getting to that moment was far more difficult than the numbers suggest. Initially, progress came relatively easily—five minutes here, seven minutes there—as I chipped away at my time. But the closer I got to the sub-60 barrier, the more elusive those final minutes became. I had countless rides where I finished agonizingly close— just a minute or ninety seconds over—each near-miss more discouraging than the last.

The transformation was complete. After years of struggle, I found myself a couple miles from the summit, the clock ticking mercilessly toward that 60-minute mark. My internal timing—honed over dozens of attempts—told me I wasn't going to make it. The familiar landmarks I'd used to gauge my progress for years were telling me I was too slow.

But something had fundamentally changed in my mind. Instead of accepting the verdict of experience, I pushed harder.

When the final stretch came into view—a particularly steep section before the finish—I rose out of the saddle, legs screaming in protest, and drove the pedals down with everything I had left. My field of vision compressed to a narrow point, the peripheral world fading away as I focused solely on the path ahead. A fierce rhythm pounded inside my chest as I willed myself forward.

Nausea surged up from my stomach into my throat. The thought flashed through my mind: If I throw up, it's going wherever it's going, because I'm not slowing down. Not now. Not this close.

I crested the final rise and frantically hit the stop button on my Garmin: 59:45. Fifteen seconds under my sub-60 goal.

Immediately, my body collected its debt. I doubled over, my breakfast violently reappearing on the asphalt. After a few gasping breaths, a second wave hit. My legs trembled so badly I had to sit on the ground next to my bike.

This wasn't just tired. This was emptied-from-the-inside-out, nothing-left-in-the-tank depletion. My guts on the asphalt, legs refusing basic commands. And right there, doubled over next to my bike, I felt something I'd never experienced before—pure, unfiltered satisfaction. The kind you can't buy or fake. The kind you only earn through complete surrender to something bigger than comfort.

The world around me widened, stretching into the valley below—a patchwork of greens and blues under the vast Utah sky. The only sounds were my ragged breathing and the distant call of a hawk riding thermals above the ridgeline—a perfect soundtrack to triumph.

With shaking hands, I pulled out my phone. The first call was to my riding buddy, who had supported this seemingly impossible goal for years.

"I did it," I managed, my voice hoarse. "Sub-sixty."

His whoop of celebration echoed through the phone. Then came calls to my wife and the small circle of people who understood what this meant—not just a bike ride, but a monument to persistence. I sat there at the summit for nearly an hour, letting the significance of the moment sink in, before beginning the descent.

I didn't just finish a bike ride that day; I redefined what I believed was possible. The limits we accept are mostly illusions. Dangerous, convincing illusions, but illusions nonetheless.

That's the secret to building 'never quit' into your DNA—you have to prove to yourself, through action, that your limits are self-imposed fiction.

Breaking that sub-60-minute barrier up that legendary route wasn't an ending—it was just the warmup. Later that same year, I'd be standing at the edge of a different challenge, one that would make those canyon battles look like casual Sunday rides. The mountain had been my teacher, but I was about to find out if I'd been a good enough student.

The Invisible Battle I Never Told Anyone About

Three months before the race, I woke before the rest of the world for a scheduled five-hour training session. As I sat on the edge of my bed, staring at my gear, doubt pressed in—not just fatigue or reluctance, but bone-deep certainty that I was fooling myself.

Time stretched as I sat frozen on the edge of my bed, trapped in a mental war that made the physical challenge ahead seem insignificant.

"Who the hell are you kidding?" the voice was relentless. 'You're not an athlete. Never have been. You're the guy who got cut from every team. The guy gasping for air after a single pool length. And now you think

you're going to swim 2.4 miles? Bike 112? Run a marathon? You're going to humiliate yourself, and for what?'

My gear sat there, mocking me. My wife slept peacefully, unaware of my internal war. I hadn't told her about these moments. Saying it out loud would make it real—would force me to admit that maybe this whole thing was just middle-aged desperation wrapped in spandex.

Something had to break. Either I was getting up, or I was crawling back under the covers and abandoning the whole endeavor.

That's when I found it—a mental move born of pure necessity. I put both palms on my knees, closed my eyes, and in my mind, repeated words that weren't pretty or profound, just true:

"This isn't about finishing. This is about finding out. And the only way to find out is to try."

I repeated it silently, over and over. Each repetition grew more insistent in my mind, drowning out the doubts. Until it was louder than the fear. Until my hands pushed off my knees and I was standing.

I'd love to tell you I strode confidently into the darkness, but the truth is I shuffled out like a man heading to the gallows. But I was moving. And movement beats perfection every single time.

This Dawn Mantra was the raw beginning of what would later evolve into more sophisticated tools for mental control. While the 5-Second Launch Code and *Pause & Pivot* techniques are refined systems, this early mantra was their origin—a primitive but powerful method for overriding the brain's instinct to keep us comfortable.

When Even Ironman Bows to Nature

For eight grueling months after signing up for the Lake Tahoe Ironman, I restructured my days around a single goal—without compromising what mattered most. This phase of my mental journey tested whether I could maintain discipline not just for a day or week, but for months of sustained effort. While many triathletes rearrange their entire lives at the expense of relationships, I made a different choice. Every morning at 4 AM, my alarm would shatter the silence while the rest of the house slept peacefully. I'd slip quietly from bed, lace up in the dark, and hit the roads or the pool before dawn broke.

This wasn't just about athletic endurance—it was a deliberate strategy to protect my family from the collateral damage of my ambition. By the time my kids stumbled sleepy-eyed into the kitchen for breakfast, I'd already completed a punishing workout and was ready to help with backpacks and lunch boxes. Weekends required longer training sessions, but I meticulously scheduled these to finish before lunchtime, preserving afternoons for soccer games and family outings.

The training was unrelenting—early morning swims in freezing pools when my body and mind screamed for more sleep, mind-numbing hours on the bike while the neighborhood still slept, solitary runs through empty streets illuminated only by streetlights. But this approach meant I didn't have to choose between being a present father and pursuing this challenge. It wasn't always perfect, but it demonstrated something crucial: extraordinary goals don't have to come at the expense of your most important relationships.

When race week finally arrived, we packed up the minivan—bike, wetsuit, running gear, mountains of nutrition, and a nervous energy I couldn't contain. The ten-hour drive to Lake Tahoe was filled with mental rehearsals of the course and quiet moments of doubt I tried to hide from my family.

Lake Tahoe stunned me with its beauty. Crystal clear water surrounded by towering pines and snow-capped mountains—a postcard setting for what would be the hardest physical challenge of my life. We rented a cabin with a view that made the months of early alarms seem worth it. Even better, my father had decided to compete in the half-Ironman happening the same weekend. Having him there transformed this personal quest into something generational—a moment we'd both remember forever.

We spent the day before the race picking up our race packets, organizing transition bags, and nervously checking and rechecking gear. That night, I went to bed early, staring at the ceiling and trying to quiet my racing mind. After months of preparation, I was finally ready.

Then, at 4 AM on race morning—a time now hardwired into my body after countless training days—I was jolted awake by what sounded like a siren. Stepping onto the cabin's deck, I noticed a thick haze had settled overnight. I couldn't see more than a few hundred feet in front of me—the mountains had vanished into a gray shroud of smoke.

Despite the ominous conditions, I went through my pre-race routine methodically. Breakfast: two plain bagels with almond butter, banana, and a cup of coffee. The rest of the house gradually stirred to life— my wife moving through her own morning routine, my dad silently preparing his own race nutrition in the kitchen. We loaded the car in relative silence, the gravity of the day settling over us.

The drive to the starting area was surreal. Headlights cut through the smoky darkness, revealing only fragments of the landscape that had been so breathtaking the day before. As we parked and unloaded our gear, we joined a stream of athletes heading toward the beach, all of us casting concerned glances at the hazy sky.

At the transition area, I methodically arranged my bike and run gear, checking and rechecking that everything was in its place. With transition set, I pulled on my wetsuit and headed to the start line. The beach was a surreal scene—hundreds of neoprene-clad athletes milling about in the pre-dawn fog, their headlamps creating eerie halos in the smoke. We kept glancing at race officials, trying to read their faces as they huddled in urgent conversation.

Just five minutes before the scheduled start, the announcement came: "Due to hazardous air quality from nearby wildfires, the 2014 Lake Tahoe Ironman has been canceled."

The beach went silent—then erupted in a confused chorus of protests and questions. I stood frozen, wetsuit half-zipped, unable to process what I was hearing. Months of predawn wake-ups, thousands of miles, countless moments of grit when no one was watching—all of it, leading to nothing.

Athletes around me broke down. Some cried openly. Others were furious. Most just stood there, shell-shocked.

I spotted my dad in the crowd, our matching race bibs a cruel reminder of what wouldn't happen today.

"That's it?" His voice caught, the disappointment hitting him in waves —just like it was hitting me. "All those early alarms. All those miles. For nothing?"

I stood there, wetsuit half on, as the thought looped in my head: *For nothing? For nothing? All of it... for nothing?*

That night, lying in the cabin listening to my family sleep, I made a decision: This setback would be nothing more than a comma in my story, not a period. I opened my laptop and searched for upcoming Ironman races. Most were either sold out or months away. Then I found it—Chattanooga, Tennessee. Just two weeks later.

Most people would consider it impossible to pivot that quickly—to recover mentally, adjust travel plans, and somehow transport a bike across the country on a budget already stretched thin by the Tahoe trip. The logistics alone seemed insurmountable.

But something in me refused to wait another year to test my limits. I registered for Chattanooga at 2 AM, closed my laptop, and finally slept—a man with a new problem to solve, but no longer a man without a purpose.

This moment of adaptation and resilience eventually evolved into a more structured approach to narrative reframing. At the time, I didn't have a framework for turning setbacks into opportunities—just an instinctive pivot from disappointment to determination. But that raw shift became the foundation for something much bigger.

Pain Reframing: The Advanced Evolution of Mental Control

The Chattanooga race presented physical and mental challenges beyond anything I'd prepared for. The most significant test came during the 112-mile bike segment, where I found myself wrestling with an unfamiliar triathlon bike, my body rebelling against the aggressive position.

For those who don't ride, let me explain something crucial: a triathlon bike is fundamentally different from a standard road bike. The geometry positions you far forward, with your weight resting on your elbows rather than your hands, and your body angled in an aggressive aerodynamic tuck. It's designed purely for speed, not comfort. I'd trained exclusively on a road bike back home—upright position, familiar handling, comfortable fit. Now I was attempting to race 112 miles on what felt like an alien machine with completely different muscle demands and handling characteristics.

It was like training for months to run a marathon in running shoes, then being handed ice skates at the starting line. My body was rebelling against this unfamiliar position almost immediately. Within the first hour, muscles I didn't even know I had were screaming in protest.

At mile 78, I hit the wall—literally. My neck muscles temporarily gave out, dropping my gaze to the pavement directly below me instead of the road ahead. By the time I registered what was happening and tried to correct course, I had veered off the road. My front wheel caught the edge of someone's mailbox, sending a jolt through the unfamiliar frame. I barely stayed upright, skidding to a stop in a stranger's front yard.

For thirty seconds, I just stood there straddling the bike, my breath coming in ragged gasps. Every instinct screamed to find a comfortable position, to let my muscles recover. The race officials driving by would never know if I rested for ten minutes. Twenty. Or if I called it quits altogether.

The scorching Tennessee sun beat down relentlessly, turning the asphalt into a griddle that radiated heat through my cycling shoes. Sweat cascaded down my face, stinging my eyes and leaving trails of salt on my skin. My heart hammered against my ribs, and my neck muscles spasmed in protest of hours spent in that unnatural position. My body wasn't just tired—it was staging a full-scale rebellion.

"You can do anything for 34 more miles," I told myself, the words coming out in a whisper. *"Just keep pedaling. The pain is information, not an emergency."*

That moment hit me with a mental game-changer I now call 'pain reframing.' I stopped seeing discomfort as something to dodge—like it was out to break me—and started treating it like raw data, proof my body was hitting its edge. By shifting my headspace to view pain as neutral intel instead of a red alert, I could face it head-on without letting it run the show.

Standing there on the side of that Tennessee road, I wasn't thinking about mental mastery frameworks or systems. But looking back, this was where everything leveled up. The 'just three more steps' thinking that had saved me on countless climbs wasn't enough anymore. This was advanced warfare—my mind needed to actually reinterpret pain, not just endure it.

I thought of my four kids back home. What would I tell them if I quit? That it got hard? That daddy gave up when things became uncomfortable?

No. That wasn't the lesson I wanted to teach them.

I climbed back on and pushed off, the mailbox serving as both a wake-up call and a metaphor—sometimes the most valuable lessons come from our most painful collisions.

The Cooper Kupp Mindset: Earning It Every Single Day—Just Like 4 AM Training

NFL receiver Cooper Kupp embodies one fundamental truth that defines greatness: you must earn success every single day—the same lesson those relentless 4 AM training sessions taught me long before dawn broke over my neighborhood.

When Kupp was a high school freshman, he weighed just 119 pounds — fully clothed and soaking wet. Coaches dismissed him. Peers ignored him. But Kupp simply focused on improving. Before school, after school, running hills in local parks, sprinting home with his mother picking up his backpack so he could run faster—he never stopped working. At no point did he feel he'd "made it" or "deserved" anything. Instead, he constantly asked himself, "How much better can I get?"

In college at Eastern Washington, Kupp encountered doubt again. Coaches murmured he'd never see the field. Instead of letting those whispers discourage him, he quietly embraced them as motivation. Every single day, he woke up determined to reflect his dreams in his actions. When he went to sleep, he evaluated his day by one simple measure: Did I do everything I could today to earn my goals?

Getting drafted into the NFL didn't change his mindset—it intensified it. Entering the NFL wasn't the finish line; it was just another starting point. Kupp continued to approach each day with relentless determination, knowing that past accomplishments entitled him to nothing. Each year he finished, he immediately set his sights higher, pushing himself to ask, "How can I improve again? How can I earn it again tomorrow?"

I recognized this same mindset in myself during those pre-dawn training sessions. There were no fans cheering, no medals at the end of each workout—just the quiet satisfaction of knowing I was earning it when no one was watching. Like Kupp, I learned that yesterday's victories buy you nothing today. You have to earn it all over again with each sunrise.

Why the Earn-It Mindset Matters

Cooper Kupp's approach reveals a fundamental principle about success: it isn't deserved, it is earned—again and again. He recognizes that entitlement destroys growth, while continuous effort fosters limitless potential. He embodies the understanding that success isn't a destination but an ongoing process of continuous improvement.

This "earn it every day" mindset forms a perfect bridge to Chapter 9's exploration of gratitude as a mental weapon. The humility inherent in having to earn your place daily creates the ideal foundation for the type of gratitude that fuels resilience rather than complacency.

The Ironman Mindset: Lessons for Every Challenge in Life

This mindset isn't just for endurance athletes. It's the same mindset that builds businesses, transforms relationships, overcomes addiction, and achieves the seemingly impossible in any arena. Here's what I learned about the 90% above the shoulders that determines everything else:

1. Transform Doubt into Rocket Fuel

When my coworker said, "You definitely couldn't do it," those words could have been a wall or a launch pad. The choice was mine. I chose to let them propel me forward.

Think about the doubts you face right now—whether from others or your own inner critic. What if those very doubts contain the energy you need to prove them wrong? Don't run from doubt—transmute it.

The words that were meant to limit you can become the very fuel that propels you beyond all expectations. The criticism that stings today can become the fire that forges your resolve tomorrow.

2. Bite-Sized Wins

Standing at the edge of the pool that first day, contemplating a 2.4-mile swim seemed absurd. So I didn't think about 2.4 miles. I thought about 25 yards. Then 50. Then 100.

That's how you'll conquer that impossible goal you identified at the beginning of this book. Don't let the magnitude paralyze you. Break it down until the first step feels trivial. Then take that step. Then another. The path to extraordinary achievement is paved with ordinary actions taken consistently.

Remember that impossible goal you wrote down in the Introduction? This is exactly how you'll conquer it—not by staring at the whole mountain, but by focusing on the next step, the next milestone, the next bite-sized win. What would be your equivalent of "25 yards, then 50, then 100" for your impossible goal? Your brain can handle these small challenges, even when the overall goal seems overwhelming.

Right now—literally right now—what massive goal are you avoiding? Don't kid yourself. You know exactly what it is. That thing that scares you just enough to keep postponing it. How could you make the first step so ridiculously small that saying no would actually feel more uncomfortable than taking action? Because that's where this game is won—making inaction more painful than action.

3. Celebrate Microscopic Wins

Two weeks into training, I managed to swim 400 yards without stopping. It wasn't impressive by any objective standard—many people can do this without training. But for me, it was a breakthrough that deserved acknowledgment.

Your brain craves evidence of progress. Feed it regularly by celebrating improvements too small for anyone else to notice. These micro-victories create the neurological foundation for the bigger breakthroughs that follow.

4. Remember the Breakthrough Threshold

The most powerful insight from my journey—the cornerstone of mental mastery—is understanding that your brain signals surrender long before you reach your actual capacity. This isn't just motivational rhetoric; it's a neurological reality that explains why most people never reach their potential.

When your mind insists you've hit your limit, remind yourself: "This is just the first threshold. My actual capacity lies beyond this point."

This *Breakthrough Threshold* applies not just to physical challenges, but to every aspect of life—from creative pursuits to professional challenges to personal growth. The voice that tells you "I can't" is almost always lying.

Your Mental Mastery Journey Continues

The Snowbird climbs and Ironman journey weren't just isolated athletic accomplishments—they formed a progressive laboratory of mental mastery where each challenge built upon the last, teaching me principles that would later evolve into the framework we've been building throughout this book:

> The raw survival instinct of "just one more pedal stroke" transformed into the systematic *Bite-Sized Wins* strategy that helps you break overwhelming challenges into manageable pieces

> Those countless hours on that mountain showed me how pushing past perceived limits physically reshapes what your mind is capable of

> The primitive "Dawn Mantra" became the foundation for taking control of your thoughts instead of letting them control you

> That abrupt pivot from Tahoe to Chattanooga taught me how to transform setbacks into opportunities by changing the story I told myself

> And that pain reframing technique on the scorching Tennessee roads? That's how I learned to disrupt negative thought patterns before they spiral out of control

And yes, I did finish the Ironman that year—crossing the finish line in Chattanooga with nothing left in the tank, just as I had when I broke the 60-minute barrier at Snowbird. The same mental framework that helped me conquer that mountain carried me through 140.6 miles of swimming, biking, and running. The venues were different, but the battle was the same—it all happened above the shoulders.

Next, we'll explore how gratitude—not as a soft, sentimental practice, but as a powerful mental weapon—can transform your relationship with challenges and accelerate your progress toward even your most impossible goals.

Remember, the same voice that tells you that you can't climb the mountain, swim across the pool, or finish the race is the same voice telling you that you can't start the business, repair the relationship, or overcome the addiction. It's the same liar, using the same playbook.

This is what building 'never quit' into your DNA really means. It's not that you never fall—it's that you always get back up.

CHAPTER 9: THE GRATITUDE HACK: A MENTAL WEAPON FOR RESILIENCE

I'd already battled wildfire cancellations, mailbox collisions, and every excuse to quit. But here's what I didn't tell you—what really dragged my sorry ass across that finish line wasn't just stubbornness.

It was straight-up gratitude.

My wife, my four kids, my family, my friends—they'd been with me every soul-draining mile, even if they weren't there in Chattanooga. Eight months of 4 AM wake-ups, me sneaking out while they slept, them cheering at soccer games I'd race back for, friends texting "You got this" when I doubted I did. They weren't just rooting for me—they were *in* it with me, every stroke, pedal, and stride. And when that finish line loomed, blurry through sweat and haze, I didn't just see pavement—I saw them. Their belief, their love, their stake in me crossing that line.

I stumbled over it, 140.6 miles done, and the crowd's roar hit like a wave. But the real moment came later, when I finally got my hands on a phone. My voice cracked as I dialed home—exhausted, raw, barely holding it together. "I did it," I managed, and the cheers through the line nearly broke me completely. My wife's proud laugh, my kids yelling over each other, friends whooping like they'd run it too—I had to choke it down, that lump in my throat, because gratitude hit harder than the race itself.

Something extraordinary happened in my brain at that moment—a flood of oxytocin and dopamine that neuroscientists call the *gratitude cascade*. This wasn't just me getting emotional. This neural firestorm was actively repairing my depleted body, killing inflammation, and rewiring my brain's response to suffering. Above the shoulders, that love turned exhaustion into something bigger—strength I didn't know I had.

That's gratitude—not some soft, sappy side note, but a steel beam in your mental frame. It's not about glossing over the hurt; it's about seeing who's got your back when it stings the most.

I've lived it, seen it in champions, and dug into the science that proves it.

This chapter is about how gratitude rewires your brain, keeps you unbreakable when life gets relentless, and turns your words into power.

Because up here, gratitude isn't a bonus—it's the bedrock of mental toughness.

The Comment That Kicked Me in the Gut

Gratitude can hit quiet and hard, like a whisper that shatters stone. When wildfires canceled the 2014 Lake Tahoe Ironman, the beach emptied fast. My dad and I trudged to the transition area, backpacks stuffed with shoes, helmets, and broken plans, our bikes rolling beside us like faithful dogs sensing our defeat. My wife snapped a photo—us lost in a defeated herd. I posted it online, half-bitter: "Now what? Can't believe this happened."

Then my cousin commented. She was younger than me, a mother of four, and dying of stage-four colon cancer. She'd fallen hard for running—said it made her feel alive. But now, with cancer draining that life dry, she typed: *"At least you can still do this."*

Five words. That's all it took.

I stood there, backpack sagging, bike steady, feeling stronger than I'd been in years—legs primed, lungs full—while she withered at her worst. She couldn't run, couldn't fight like me, and I was whining about a detour? Above the shoulders, it flipped: this wasn't a loss—it was a gift I'd nearly missed. Two weeks later, crossing Chattanooga's finish line—bruised from that mailbox crash, wrestling a rental bike that hated me—I heard her echo in every step. Gratitude didn't erase the grind; it turned it into proof I was still here. A lesson she taught me as she faded.

This isn't just a touching story—it's gratitude as a weapon, reshaping how your brain processes setbacks. My cousin's comment didn't minimize the disappointment. It completely reframed it—shifted my focus from what I'd lost to what I still had. That's the hack—not denying the crap but seeing it surrounded by gifts you're overlooking.

The Crash That Taught Me to See Differently

On a flawless June day, after summiting Little Cottonwood Canyon to Snowbird with three friends—the same punishing climb I took you through just a chapter ago—I began the descent. This was my victory lap. The exhilarating reward for the climb. A route I'd done nearly 100 times before.

Then, disaster struck.

A car pulled out directly in my path as I flew down the canyon at nearly highway speed. I had a split-second choice: plow into its rear and risk shattering through the windshield or veer off the shoulder onto loose gravel.

I chose the dirt.

Time stretched. I felt the slip, fought for balance, then tumbled violently in a blur of flesh, carbon fiber, and asphalt.

When I stopped rolling, half my kit was shredded, my elbow split open with a chunk of arm seemingly missing, and blood dripped off my fingertips in rhythmic drops. My hip and leg looked like I'd slid into second base over a cheese grater. Gravel embedded itself in my palms. My world spun in kaleidoscopic fragments as shock numbed me.

And yet, as I sat there—bleeding, broken, and disoriented—one detail cut through the chaos.

A single wildflower, growing from a crack in the asphalt.

In that moment, gratitude shifted my perspective before my body even felt the pain. I had survived. I was still conscious. I wasn't paralyzed. And though I was about to be rushed to the hospital, my worst-case scenario had not come true

That flower, absurdly delicate in such a harsh setting, was a reminder: even in moments of destruction, life persists.

Recovery was its own mountain to climb. The physical healing took weeks—stitches, road rash, muscles locked from trauma. But the mental recovery was the real challenge.

I had two choices:

> Let fear dictate my future.
>
> Find gratitude in what remained.

At first, I struggled. My bike was totaled, and honestly, I wasn't ready to get back on one anyway. But I wouldn't let the mountain win. So I started running the canyon instead—same roads, same views, just on my own two feet. Every time I hit that section of road, the memory of that crash flooded my body with hesitation. The fear was real. But so was the lesson from the wildflower.

My wife, sensing my struggle, questioned even this approach.

"You almost died on that mountain," she said the night before my first canyon run, her voice tight with worry. "Is proving something to yourself worth risking everything?"

I considered her words carefully.

"It's not about proving something," I finally replied. "It's about not letting fear make my decisions. The moment I let fear win, it never stops winning."

The crash had taken something from me—not just skin and blood, but a certain fearlessness.

Yet in its place came something more valuable: gratitude for my body, gratitude for my mind's ability to rebuild, and gratitude for the lessons found in the struggle.

The Science: Why Gratitude Works (Hint: It's Not What You Think)

Picture this: You're locked in standstill traffic, already twenty minutes late, watching the minutes tick by on your dashboard. Some guy in a luxury SUV just cut you off to gain exactly one car length. Your brain's flooding with cortisol—stress hormone surging through your bloodstream—and your amygdala's lighting up like Times Square, screaming "Everything is falling apart!" That's your default setting when life kicks you in the teeth.

But what if you flipped the script? What if, instead of *"This day is ruined,"* you thought, *"At least I've got a reliable car, a podcast I love, and a chance to take some deep breaths before this meeting"*?

Sounds simple, maybe even a little cheesy. But here's the dirty little secret: gratitude doesn't just make you feel better—it physically reshapes your brain's architecture. This isn't separate from the neuroplasticity we saw with those London cabbies back in Chapter 2. It's the same principle in action. Every time you choose gratitude over complaint, you're literally carving new neural pathways that change how your brain processes challenges.

Researchers at UCLA put people under fMRI machines and watched in real-time as gratitude practices fired up the prefrontal cortex— your brain's command center that keeps you calm when everything goes to hell. At the same time, it triggers a flood of dopamine and serotonin, neurochemicals that basically drown out stress hormones like a fire hose on a match.

Think of it like this: You know when your phone freezes up and you have to do a hard reset? Gratitude is that for your brain—except instead of just restarting the same operating system, it installs an upgrade that makes you crash-resistant.

One study showed that just eight weeks of daily gratitude practice— three minutes each morning—slashed cortisol levels by 23% and significantly boosted resilience under pressure. The control group showed no changes whatsoever. This isn't wishful thinking—it's hardware modification for your brain.

When I lost my entire manuscript, my initial reaction was pure amygdala hijack—panic, doom, catastrophizing.

But when I shifted to gratitude—*"I still have all the ideas and insights in my head"*—my prefrontal cortex regained control, cortisol levels dropped, and clarity cut through the fog of panic.

That's not spiritual bypassing; that's your brain's wiring responding to your mindset. Gratitude isn't a Band-Aid over a bullet wound; it's a hard reset above the shoulders, flipping your brain from survival mode to strength mode. And the more you practice it, the more automatic it becomes—neuroplasticity at work, carving new neural highways that don't buckle when life throws its worst at you.

Gratitude becomes especially powerful when you hit your *Breakthrough Threshold*—that moment when your brain screams it's time to quit.

By redirecting your focus to appreciation instead of discomfort, you're hacking your brain's governor system and unlocking access to reserves you didn't even know you had.

The Champions: How Gratitude Fuels the Elite

Ever wonder how the greatest stay unbreakable when everything's collapsing? It's not just grit or talent—gratitude is their secret fuel, a fire that burns through the darkest moments.

Alex Kopacz knew this feeling. He battled pneumonia on his way to Olympic gold—then later faced a life-threatening illness that pinned him down. *"I'd lie in that hospital bed,"* he told me, voice rasping through the phone, faint but fierce, *"and think, 'I'm still here. I've still got a shot.'"*

Tubes snaked from his arms, oxygen mask hissing—yet gratitude kept his mind sharp when his body failed. It dragged him back, step by painful step, to his home gym, rebuilding that championship strength.

And Kopacz isn't alone. Ashley Caldwell—who fought through five career-threatening injuries—built her Olympic gold on the same fire. When I asked how she kept pushing forward, she flashed that characteristic grin and said with absolute conviction: *"Every day I could still ski, even hobbling in pain, was a gift. You don't quit on a gift."*

Those exact words—you don't quit on a gift—capture the essence of how gratitude transforms our relationship with challenge. It's not about denying the hard stuff or pretending it doesn't hurt.

It's about seeing the hard stuff as proof that you're still in the fight—still worthy of the struggle. This power of gratitude isn't limited to elite athletics—I've experienced its transformative effect in my professional life as well. For years, I thought I was invisible at work— pouring my guts into marketing plans, photo shoots, athlete interviews, and getting nothing back. No nod, no "nice job," just silence. Resentment took root fast—small gripes to my wife turned into full-on rants, my nights spent stewing, neck locked tight, convinced I deserved more. It wasn't just a mood; it was a cage I'd built above the shoulders, every bar forged from what I wasn't getting.

That grind nearly broke me. I'd spent weeks perfecting a campaign for our biggest event of the year—pouring over every detail until 2AM most nights—only to hear crickets when it launched. But here's the side I didn't tell you: the gratitude that pulled me out wasn't some grand epiphany—it was a quiet gut punch. One night, staring at the ceiling, I stopped counting slights and started counting what I had. They'd handed me a gig I wasn't ready for—raw trust in a guy with more hustle than credentials. That hit different. Not shame, not a fix, just a flicker of "damn, I'm lucky they took a chance on me."

That night, I didn't just type that email to say thanks—I *felt* it in my bones. My fingers shook, not from nerves, but from something shifting loose. When I hit send, it wasn't about them—it was about me. My shoulders dropped, the vise on my chest cracked open, and the darkness around me didn't feel so suffocating. The truth couldn't wait until morning—it needed to be captured while this moment of clarity was still raw and real.

After sending that message, I felt a weight lift from my shoulders— literally. The tension that had been building in my neck and back for months began to release. I wasn't chasing applause anymore; I was standing on ground I'd forgotten was solid. Within weeks, my creative output doubled—not because I was working more hours, but because I was working from gratitude instead of resentment. Gratitude didn't erase the work—it rewrote how I carried it. Above the shoulders, it turned a weight into a win, not because the load lightened, but because I got stronger.

The performance impact of this mindset shift is undeniable. I witnessed this firsthand during my Ironman training. After implementing a structured gratitude practice during those grueling swims, I shaved nearly two minutes off my mile time in just under two months—with no changes to my physical training approach. The transformation came from how gratitude shifted my relationship with suffering.

During those endless laps, instead of fighting the burning in my shoulders and lungs, I started actively thanking my body: "Thank you for being strong enough to feel this pain." The discomfort didn't disappear, but it transformed from my enemy into valuable feedback —data that I was pushing my limits and growing stronger.

This isn't just for athletes—it works in every arena of human achievement. The way we perceive our experiences—through gratitude or complaint—reshapes us down to our cells.

The Words That Shape Our Reality

The words you choose—especially those you speak to yourself—have profound effects on your physical and mental state. And it's not just psychological. Researchers in psychoneuroimmunology have proven that our internal dialogue directly impacts our nervous system, stress hormones, and even immune function.

After my bike wreck, I road-tested this exact approach. Laid out on my couch, elbow stitched together, arm looking like something from a horror movie, my first thought was: *"Season's done. All that training wasted."* Instant physical response—shoulders locked up, breathing went shallow, whole body tensed like it was bracing for more impact.

Then I caught myself. Switched the internal dialogue: *"Thanks for the reminder I'm tougher than I think. Lucky to still have all my parts attached."* Not some fake positive BS—a genuine recognition that despite the pain, I had something real to appreciate. Twenty seconds later? Shoulders dropped. Jaw unclenched. Breathing deepened. Same injuries, completely different physical state—all from shifting what was happening above the shoulders.

Dr. Richard Davidson at the University of Wisconsin-Madison has documented how positive emotional states induced through practices like gratitude create measurable changes in brain activity patterns and immune response. In one study, participants who engaged in gratitude practices showed increased activity in the medial prefrontal cortex—a region associated with positive emotion regulation—and reduced inflammatory markers in blood tests.

The practical application is dead simple: The words you speak aren't just expressing how you feel—they're programming your biological systems for either chaotic disruption or peak performance.

The Practice: Three No-BS Moves to Build a Grateful Mind

You don't need a lab coat or an Olympic medal to make gratitude work in your life—it's street-level, do-it-now stuff that delivers results regardless of your circumstances. Here's how I've hardwired it into my daily existence, and how you can too. These aren't fluffy journal prompts or feel-good exercises; they're battle-tested mental tools that strengthen your mind precisely when it wants to cave.

1. The Three-Win Wake-Up

The 5-Second Launch Code helps you program your brain's filter the moment you wake up—with declarations like *"I'm unstoppable today."*

Now, we're going to supercharge that morning mental programming by layering in gratitude.

The Three-Win Wake-Up builds on your Launch Code foundation. The Launch Code gives your mind direction. The Three-Win Wake-

Up adds fuel — real, daily appreciation that keeps your mindset grounded and your momentum growing.

Here's how to integrate these complementary techniques:

First, as soon as you wake up, implement your 5-Second Launch Code with a powerful declaration: "I'm unstoppable today" or "I own this day."

Then, immediately follow with the Three-Win Wake-Up by identifying three specific things you're genuinely grateful for. But these aren't vague platitudes—they're concrete, gritty details from your life. Not "I'm grateful to be alive," but "My legs still ache from yesterday's ride—that means they're working hard and getting stronger." Or "My kid laughed at my ridiculous dad joke last night—we still have that connection."

This one-two combination creates a powerful neurological effect: your Launch Code activates your brain's achievement centers, while your Three-Win gratitude practice triggers the release of dopamine and serotonin, creating biochemical reinforcement of your positive mindset.

By stacking these techniques, you're not just programming your brain's filter—you're creating an emotional foundation that makes you virtually bulletproof against the day's challenges.

This 30-second practice specifically directs your brain's Reticular Activating System to scan for positive evidence throughout your day. The key is specificity and authenticity. Your brain knows when you're just going through the motions, so don't fake it.

Try it tomorrow morning—name three genuine gratitudes out loud, and feel the immediate shift. It's like flipping the switch from "scanning for problems" to "scanning for opportunities" before your day even starts.

2. The Shovel Switch

Remember my Utah winter meltdown? I absolutely hated shoveling snow—back-breaking, soul-crushing misery that seemed to go on forever. Until I deliberately flipped the narrative: "This snow is my ticket to perfect powder on the slopes." The physical labor didn't change, but my experience of it transformed completely.

This real-time gratitude pivot uses the same mental machinery as cognitive reframing, but with a critical difference—instead of just stopping a negative spiral, you're actively replacing it with appreciation. Now, mid-dread—shoveling, tough calls, fierce workouts—I flip it:

"This resistance builds mental calluses I'll need later."

"This uncomfortable conversation solves something important."

"This pain proves my body's getting stronger."

Find one genuine thing your personal "winter" is giving you—say it out loud, mean it in your bones—and watch how your experience shifts. Don't just try this during easy moments. The real power comes when you're mid-suffering and can flip the script live, in real-time.

3. The Nighttime Reset

Before bed, when most people reach for their phones to scroll mindlessly, I grab mine for a different purpose: to jot down one specific moment from the day I'm genuinely thankful for. Could be seemingly insignificant: "The coffee was perfect—right when I needed it most." Could be profound: "I finally broke through on that impossible chapter."

This one-minute practice is the perfect bookend to the thought-debugging tools you've already built. While those techniques help you break negative spirals once they've started, this nighttime gratitude ritual prevents rumination before it can take hold. It's like installing a firewall against the negative loops that typically hijack your mind when your head hits the pillow. One night I wrote, "Kopacz called—still kicking ass post-illness," and instantly felt my shoulders drop away from my ears.

What makes this practice so powerful is how it hacks your brain's nighttime processing. Your brain doesn't just shut down when you sleep—it's actively sorting through the day's experiences, strengthening connections it deems important. By focusing on gratitude right before bed, you're essentially telling your brain, "Hey, this is the stuff worth remembering." Your brain spends the night cementing these grateful thoughts into your neural pathways, making them more readily accessible the next day.

Sleep researcher Dr. Robert Stickgold at Harvard confirmed this, finding that what you focus on before sleep gets VIP treatment during REM cycles. You're literally programming your mind for resilience while you rest, building up reserves you'll draw from when life punches you in the face tomorrow.

These aren't chores—they're mental reps, as crucial as any physical training. Like lifting weights, the first few gratitude practices might feel awkward or forced. But stick with it, and your brain starts craving the neurochemical hit—dopamine firing, cortisol fading, resilience stacking up day by day. I'm no guru; I'm just a guy who's learned through pain and research that gratitude is a muscle, and flexing it daily keeps me standing when life swings its hardest punches.

The Fight Above the Shoulders

Gratitude isn't soft—it's a gut punch to despair. It's Kopacz in his hospital bed thanking his lungs for still drawing breath when doctors weren't sure they would. It's me staring at a wildflower through blood-blurred vision after a bike crash that should have broken me.

It's you, right now, finding one thing in your mess of a day that's worth acknowledging.

The science says it works. Champions live by it. I've tested it in my toughest moments and found it true: gratitude changes your brain, your energy, your physical reality. It's not about pretending life is perfect—it's about seeing the cracks as proof you're still here, still in the fight. Above the shoulders, gratitude isn't just a feeling; it's your shield when life tries to break you and your sword when you need to break through.

Pick up this practice daily, and watch how it rewires everything over the long haul. Start small. Start now. Start with whatever's in front of you.

As we move into the next chapter on handling change and uncertainty, you'll discover how these gratitude practices become your stabilizing force when everything around you turns to chaos. Mental resilience isn't just about enduring difficulty—it's about transforming how you experience it.

So, what's your "thanks" today? Say it out loud. Not as some spiritual exercise, but as a neurological intervention. Because in this unrelenting fight called life, gratitude is the move that keeps you standing when everything else is telling you to fall—tougher, sharper, unbreakable.

PART III

ADAPTING, GROWING, AND THRIVING

CHAPTER 10: HOW TO HANDLE CHANGE AND UNCERTAINTY LIKE A PRO

The Shift I Didn't See Coming

I still remember the exact moment uncertainty hit me like a freight train. There I was, lying in a hotel room bed in Charlotte, North Carolina, at 11:47 PM. My wife and kids were finally asleep after the cross-country drive, but I was wide awake—a relentless pounding filled my chest, sweat beading on my forehead despite the cranked AC. The digital clock's red numbers pulsed with my racing thoughts, casting an eerie glow across the unfamiliar room.

The decision had made perfect sense back in Utah. We'd been comfortable—*too* comfortable. The same restaurants, the same hiking trails, the same family rhythms for years. That comfort had started feeling like a bubble—one that was quietly limiting our growth, just like a fixed mindset can.

When my company supported remote work, my wife and I saw an opportunity. We gathered our four kids around the dining table and laid out the pros and cons of a cross-country move.

Together, we made the bold choice to pop that comfort bubble—to experience new cultures, new landscapes, new challenges that would help us all grow.

But now, 2,000 miles from everything familiar, doubt crashed over me in waves. What if I'd pushed too far? What if the comfort bubble had popped so violently it caused trauma? I'd uprooted my entire family on this vision of growth through challenge. In the darkness of that hotel room, that decision felt less like courage and more like recklessness.

My throat tightened. My stomach knotted. The room felt like it was closing in. *"What had I done?"*

Yet by morning, something had shifted. I woke up with unexpected excitement—genuinely fired up about the adventure ahead. Same situation, same uncertainties, but a completely different experience of them. That's when I realized that uncertainty isn't just about what's happening around you—it's about what's happening above the shoulders.

This wasn't just about a move—it was the *1% Solution* in action. We'd deliberately chosen discomfort as a path to growth, applying the same principles that had shaped my mental resilience during the desert race and mountain climbs.

What started as a simple desire for change had become a real-world laboratory for testing everything I'd been building above the shoulders.

Some people crumble under uncertainty, while others thrive on it. In this chapter, we'll explore why uncertainty hits everyone differently and the exact techniques you can use to handle change like a pro— no matter your age, background, or starting point. Because in a world that never stops shifting, uncertainty isn't something to survive—it's something to master.

The Fear-to-Fuel Transformation

Uncertainty triggers an ancient response deep in your brain. Your amygdala—that walnut-sized fear factory we explored in Chapter 4—floods your system with stress hormones like cortisol and adrenaline. Your heart races. Your breathing shallows. Your thinking narrows to tunnel vision. That's not a defect; it's your brain's survival mechanism working exactly as designed: preparing you to fight or run from danger.

But here's what separates those who crack under pressure from those who conquer it: how quickly they recover from that initial spike of fear, and what meaning they assign to it.

Most people assume the solution is confidence—that bulletproof sense of *"I've got this."* But confidence can be fickle, disappearing precisely when you need it most. The real game-changer isn't eliminating fear—it's your relationship with it. Do you let fear paralyze you, or do you use it as intelligence pointing toward growth?

This transformation isn't new—it's the next evolution of the reframing techniques you've been building all along. You've already learned how to transform limiting narratives and break negative thought loops. This is that same mental machinery, now applied to uncertainty—the ultimate proving ground for everything you've built above the shoulders.

I experienced this distinction vividly at the Spartan World Championship in Lake Tahoe, when an overwhelming cold front rolled in the day before the race. Race officials announced that a mountain pond obstacle—usually just an uncomfortable swim—was now dangerously cold, making it optional. Around me, competitors groaned and strategized about skipping it.

My heart raced at the thought of that icy plunge, but something clicked in my mind. I saw the conditions differently: the harsher, the better. While others dreaded the forecast, I caught myself actually getting excited: *Bring on the snow. The tougher this gets, the better—it separates the truly committed from everyone else.* The same conditions others feared became something I almost hoped for, a mindset shift that gave me a mental edge before the race even began.

The next day at Tahoe, I stripped down to my shorts at the pond's edge, skin already prickling with goosebumps from the frigid mountain air. The water looked like liquid ice. But instead of hesitating, I dove headfirst while others remained on shore, deliberating.

The shock was immediate—the cold stole my breath and sent pain shooting through every nerve ending. But what happened next was unexpected. As I emerged from the water, instead of feeling drained, my body surged with energy. The cold plunge had triggered a flood of endorphins and adrenaline, creating a natural high that sharpened my focus and revitalized my muscles. I felt more awake, more capable than before the obstacle. What others avoided as punishment became my secret advantage—a mid-race boost that carried me through the next several miles with renewed vigor.

This taught me two powerful lessons about what happens above the shoulders: First, how we mentally frame challenges completely transforms our experience of them—seeing the cold as a storytelling opportunity rather than a threat. And second, the very discomfort we avoid often contains hidden physiological benefits we can't anticipate until we commit. The obstacle others circumvented became my competitive edge not just because I completed it, but because of the unexpected energy surge it provided.

That's the difference between those who master challenging conditions and those mastered by them. Not the absence of discomfort, but the relationship with it—both mentally reframing it as an opportunity and physically discovering how it can become fuel rather than friction.

This systematic approach to transforming uncertainty into advantage isn't something that happens by accident—it's a deliberate process you can master through the five-step Uncertainty Mastery Plan I'll share next. The same strategies that helped me transform that icy plunge from threat to advantage can help you navigate any uncertainty you face.

Your Five-Step Uncertainty Mastery Plan

Based on everything we've built throughout this book—from resilience to mindset control to narrative mastery—I've developed a five-step system for adapting to change that works whether you're facing a minor disruption or a life-altering transition. This isn't a separate framework—it's the specialized application of our *Mental Mastery Pyramid* to the specific challenge of uncertainty.

Step 1: Build Your Uncertainty Tolerance Through Deliberate Discomfort

Just as physical strength comes from progressively challenging your muscles, mental adaptability comes from gradually exposing yourself to uncertainty.

This is the essence of *Deliberate Discomfort*—training your brain through intentional challenge.

When my family and I decided to move across the country, we were deliberately choosing discomfort as a path to growth. We could have stayed in our comfortable Utah bubble—the familiar restaurants, the well-worn hiking trails, the same routine that had served us well for years. But we recognized that real growth happens at the edge of comfort, not in its center.

Your brain physically responds to this training. Just as London's cab drivers literally expanded their hippocampus by navigating challenging routes, your brain builds new neural pathways when facing uncertainty, making future adaptability easier. Each small victory in uncertainty lays down fresh neural networks that make the next challenge less threatening.

Start your own uncertainty training with the 30-Day Challenge: Each day for a month, do one small thing outside your comfort zone. It could be striking up a conversation with a stranger, trying a new hobby, or speaking up in a meeting. The size of the challenge matters less than the consistency.

Step 2: Ground Yourself When Uncertainty Hits

That first morning in Charlotte, the transformation was remarkable. I went from nighttime anxiety to morning excitement—a perfect example of how quickly your mental state can shift when you have the right framework in place. Instead of jumping straight into unpacking, I took a moment to appreciate this shift and reinforce it with a technique I now share with everyone facing uncertainty.

Remember the *Pause & Pivot* technique? When applied in uncertain situations, it becomes even more powerful.

The pause interrupts your amygdala's automatic fear response, creating just enough space for your prefrontal cortex to regain control.

The pivot then redirects your attention toward possibility instead of threat.

In uncertainty situations, I enhance this technique by deliberately engaging my senses—feeling the solid floor beneath my feet, focusing on my breathing, noticing the details of my new environment. This sensory grounding immediately pulls me out of catastrophic thinking and into the present moment.

This simple practice, which takes less than 30 seconds, creates that critical space between stimulus and response—the key to mental control.

It's not about eliminating uncertainty. It's about changing your relationship to it.

Step 3: Reframe the Story You're Telling Yourself

How you interpret uncertainty dramatically affects how you experience it. This builds directly on the narrative rewriting process we explored in Chapter 4—changing the story completely transforms your relationship with challenging situations.

Our family move to Charlotte embodied this reframing, but we didn't perfect it immediately. There were moments during those first few months that required deliberate mental shifts. When my youngest couldn't sleep in the unfamiliar house, we reframed midnight wake-ups as opportunities for special one-on-one time. When new work challenges arose—not difficulties, but opportunities to apply my skills in a fresh context—I saw them as chances to demonstrate value in new ways. My remote work arrangement actually enhanced my productivity, and since 80% of my job involved working with people outside the company, the transition made perfect sense professionally.

This progressive reframing worked with physical challenges too. When I lost the Lake Tahoe Ironman to wildfire cancellation, my first thought was *"Eight months of training wasted."* By reframing it as *"A chance to test my adaptability,"* I transformed a crushing disappointment into a new challenge. The reframing didn't eliminate the disappointment, but it gave me a constructive path forward rather than a dead end.

For Overthinkers: Emotional Differentiation

If you're prone to overthinking—as I was during that long hotel night in Charlotte—add these specialized techniques to your reframing practice:

1. Label the emotion precisely

Instead of "I feel bad," identify exactly what you're feeling: "I'm experiencing anxiety about this upcoming change." Research shows that labeling emotions with specificity immediately reduces their intensity by activating your prefrontal cortex.

2. Treat emotions as data, not directives

When uncertainty triggers fear or anxiety, view those feelings as information to consider, not commands to obey. Ask, "What is this emotion telling me that might be useful?"

3. Create emotional distance through language

When caught in emotional overwhelm, switch from "I am anxious" to "I am experiencing anxiety." This subtle shift creates space between you and the emotion, preventing it from consuming your identity.

Try the Puzzle Exercise: Take a current uncertainty in your life and write down three ways it could be an opportunity rather than just a challenge. For example, an unexpected job change might offer:

The chance to develop new skills

Exposure to a different industry or role

Freedom from aspects of your previous position that weren't fulfilling

This isn't about toxic positivity or denying genuine difficulties. It's about expanding your perspective to include possibilities alongside problems, giving your brain more options for adaptive response.

Step 4: Take Decisive Action Despite Incomplete Information

Uncertainty often triggers analysis paralysis—the tendency to keep gathering information and weighing options rather than taking action. But mastering change requires something counterintuitive: decisive movement with incomplete information.

I learned this during my Ironman journey when the Lake Tahoe race was canceled due to wildfires. That night, I felt the same stomach-churning uncertainty I'd experienced in that Charlotte hotel room. But instead of lying awake with racing thoughts, I channeled that energy into immediate action. With the event I'd trained eight months for suddenly gone, I had a choice: spend weeks researching the perfect alternative, or act immediately with the limited information I had. I chose action, signing up for the Chattanooga Ironman just two weeks later, even though I knew almost nothing about the course and would have to scramble for logistics.

When I clicked "register" for Chattanooga, something shifted—the very uncertainty that had paralyzed me became fuel for problem-solving. The action didn't eliminate the unknowns, but it transformed them from obstacles into challenges to navigate. That forward momentum carried me through the race itself, where I faced the unknown rental bike and unfamiliar course not with dread but with determination.

This action step applies the *Three More Steps* principle—breaking paralyzing challenges into manageable forward progress.

It's how you bring resilience into uncertainty, step by step, no matter how unclear the path feels.

The Action Despite Uncertainty technique helps overcome analysis paralysis:

1. Identify the smallest meaningful action you can take right now

2. Set a clear deadline for taking that action (hours, not days)

3. Execute before your mind can generate new reasons to hesitate

Remember: in uncertain situations, imperfect action beats perfect inaction every time. Your brain craves certainty before moving, but training yourself to act despite this discomfort builds the hallmark quality of uncertainty masters.

Step 5: Build Your Crew for Navigational Support

No one masters uncertainty alone. Even the most adaptive individuals rely on a carefully curated crew to provide perspective, support, and challenge during times of change.

When I moved my family to Charlotte, the transition would have overwhelmed me without my wife's steadying presence and my kids' resilience. By making the decision together around our dining table —weighing pros and cons as a unit—we created shared ownership of both the challenge and the opportunity. Their perspectives expanded my own, turning what could have been a solo struggle into a shared adventure.

The 25-Foot Rule in Action

Research shows that if you sit within 25 feet of a high performer, your own performance improves by 15%. But if you sit within 25 feet of a low performer, your performance drops by 30%. This proximity effect is especially powerful during uncertainty because your brain is constantly seeking cues about how to respond.

During my career transition from production to sports marketing, I didn't rely on a single mentor—I created my own support system. I devoured YouTube videos, studied industry articles, and strategically built relationships with people already established in the field. This self-directed approach to learning and connection-building became another form of the 25-Foot Rule in action—I deliberately put myself in proximity to the knowledge and people who could elevate my performance. Their ways of approaching challenges became contagious, lowering my own stress response and expanding my vision of what was possible.

Your ideal uncertainty crew should include:

A Realist who grounds you with truth when emotions cloud judgment

A Visionary who helps you see opportunities in the midst of chaos

A Steady Hand whose calm presence doesn't waver when things get rough

A Questioner who challenges your assumptions and helps you see blind spots

Together, these different perspectives broaden your field of view when stress and uncertainty try to narrow it, giving you access to options and insights you might miss on your own.

Uncertainty Mastery in Action: The Olympic Moment

South Korean ice dancer Yura Min faced the ultimate uncertainty test during the 2018 Winter Olympics in PyeongChang. Just seconds into her short dance routine in the team event, a hook on her costume came undone, threatening to expose her in front of millions of viewers.

"The second I turned backward, the wind hit my back, and my top started slipping," she told me later. Most athletes would panic, but Yura laughed internally at the absurdity, creating emotional distance. "I visualize everything from falls to equipment failures, so when my costume hook came loose, it wasn't completely unexpected," she shared, a testament to years of training with simulated disruptions, like holding her costume in place during practice, preparing her for chaos.

During the malfunction, she focused on her breath, feeling the ice beneath her skates, grounding herself to stay present. She reframed it as a puzzle, thinking, *"This is just another challenge; I've faced worse,"* and adjusted her movements, keeping arms higher to hold the costume, continuing without hesitation. Commentators noted, "She's handling it like a pro," and judges later praised her professionalism.

Her partnership with her skating partner formed a support system that amplified her resilience, perfectly illustrating the 25-Foot Rule we discussed earlier. They completed their routine, scoring 51.97 points and placing 9th. Post-Olympics, Yura continued her skating career while sharing her experiences with aspiring skaters. "At the end of the day, it could have been a lot worse," she reflected to me later, embodying that perfect balance of acknowledging challenges while not being defined by them.

While few of us will perform on Olympic ice, all of us face moments when something "comes undone" in our professional or personal lives, requiring the same mental presence Yura displayed. The unexpected client objection in a critical presentation, the technology failure during your talk, the family emergency that disrupts carefully laid plans—these are our Olympic moments, opportunities to demonstrate the same uncertainty mastery on our own stage.

Your Call to Action: Making Peace with Fear

Handling uncertainty like a pro isn't about eliminating fear—it's about transforming your relationship with it. As 50 Cent and Robert Greene explain in The 50th Law: "Fear is the greatest barrier to success. Those who learn to embrace it, rather than run from it, become unstoppable."

This insight mirrors everything we've been building—resilience, mindset strength, and narrative control.

Mastering uncertainty means learning to see fear not as an enemy to defeat, but as intelligence pointing toward growth.

Sometimes the most powerful growth comes from uncertainty we deliberately choose, like our family's move to Charlotte. Other times, it comes from uncertainty thrust upon us, like a race-day obstacle or a sudden change in plans. Either way, the principles for mastering it remain the same.

Choose one technique from this chapter to implement this week:

Start the 30-Day Challenge of daily comfort zone stretching

Practice the *Pause & Pivot* technique when uncertainty triggers anxiety

Apply the Puzzle Exercise to reframe a current uncertainty

Use the Action Despite Uncertainty technique on a decision you've been postponing

Begin assembling your uncertainty crew with one trusted perspective-giver

Start where you are, but start.

As you integrate these uncertainty mastery techniques into your daily life, you'll start to notice something shift. Challenges that once felt threatening begin to reveal themselves as catalysts for growth.

The mental muscles you're building now won't just help you navigate change—they'll form the foundation for the powerful habit systems we're about to explore.

Years after our move, there are still things we miss about Utah. But those gaps have been filled—with new experiences, deeper connection, and parts of ourselves we might never have discovered otherwise.

That's the real power of mastering uncertainty: it transforms what most people avoid into the very thing that shapes who you're becoming.

Whether it was losing my manuscript or crossing that Ironman finish line, I've learned that the moments that feel like breakdowns are often disguised breakthroughs—if you have the courage to lean in.

Your life's most meaningful growth isn't waiting beyond uncertainty.

It's waiting *within* it.

CHAPTER 11: THE POWER OF HABITS—YOUR BRAIN'S SHORTCUT TO SUCCESS

I t's 2 AM in a dimly lit editing suite, deadline breathing down my neck. The footage is a mess, my eyes burning, but I keep going—not because of willpower, but because of a small habit I'd built over years: organizing clips systematically before every session. That tiny routine is turning chaos into clarity now, just as habits have transformed my life's toughest challenges into victories—from crossing Ironman finish lines to writing the book you're holding.

Picture your brain as a film studio—a high-powered production house capable of creating blockbusters, if only it had the right script, crew, and direction. Most of us are stuck in pre-production limbo, running on outdated scripts: habits that lead to endless reshoots, energy-draining loops, and storylines that keep us trapped in self-doubt. But what if you could direct your own mental script—a set of habits that harnesses your brain's natural wiring to produce a life of success, scene by scene?

This chapter marks our ascent to the eleventh layer of our *Mental Mastery Pyramid*—AUTOMATION: HABIT SYSTEMS. We're now transitioning from uncertainty mastery to the automatic behaviors that ensure consistent results regardless of circumstances. While resilience gave us the foundation to persist, the mental forge strengthened our cognitive capacity, and uncertainty mastery taught us to adapt to change, habit systems transform conscious effort into unconscious excellence—creating the invisible rails that guide your success even when motivation fails or challenges multiply.

While the Five-Step Uncertainty Mastery Plan equipped you to adapt to changing circumstances, the habit systems we're about to explore will create automatic behaviors that function reliably even during those uncertain periods—transforming the Fear-to-Fuel energy we developed into consistent, productive action. Think of habits as the stabilizing force that makes uncertainty manageable through predictable routines.

For years, I dreamed of writing this book you're holding, but I'd fail repeatedly, relying on fleeting motivation—until I applied the same production mindset that saved countless film projects. I broke the massive goal into tiny, manageable scenes, setting dedicated time for writing, research, and outlining with specific deadlines, much like the daily reps that got Alex Ferreira to the Olympic podium.

This chapter isn't about trendy productivity hacks or overnight transformations. It's about understanding why habits are the brain's shortcut to success, how they've carried me through moments of doubt and exhaustion, and how you can build them to achieve the "impossible" goal you wrote down in the introduction. We'll explore the neuroscience behind habit formation, why consistent action trumps intelligence or willpower, and how to craft habits that stick— even when motivation vanishes.

The Neuroscience Behind Habit Formation: Your Brain's Hidden Superpower

Let's start with what's happening above the shoulders when you repeat an action day after day. Habits aren't magic—they're biology.

Every time you perform a behavior, your brain's basal ganglia—a cluster of neurons deep in your gray matter—takes note. It's like the editing room of a film studio where scenes are cut together into seamless sequences.

The basal ganglia starts building a loop: a cue triggers the behavior, the behavior delivers a reward, and over time, that loop becomes automatic. Neuroscientists call this the "habit loop," and it's why you can tie your shoes or brush your teeth without thinking twice. It's also why the London cabbies we met earlier could rewire their brains through repetition, expanding their hippocampus with each memorized route—a testament to the brain's plasticity we've been exploring throughout our journey together.

In 2012, MIT researchers Charles Duhigg and Ann Graybiel published groundbreaking studies on this process, showing that once a habit forms, the brain reduces its cognitive load. You stop deliberating; you just act. It's why I don't have to psych myself up to start organizing footage—it's as automatic as calling "Action!" on set. The prefrontal cortex, your brain's decision-making CEO (or film director, if you will), steps back, and the basal ganglia takes the wheel. This efficiency is your brain's way of conserving energy for bigger battles —like tackling that "Hill of Horrors" dune or rewriting the limiting narratives that hold us back.

But here's the flip side: bad habits wire themselves into your brain the same way. Early in my film career, stress on set would trigger a destructive habit: procrastinating on edits by endlessly tweaking minor details, which left me scrambling at deadlines. That loop— stress (cue) led to perfectionist tweaking (behavior), which gave me a false sense of productivity (reward)—played automatically until I recognized it and deliberately rewired it. The good news? Neuroplasticity means you can overwrite those loops with better ones, just as we saw earlier with gratitude practices that reshaped my emotional baseline.

Why Success Isn't One Big Leap—But Thousands of Small, Daily Actions

Now that we understand how the brain's editing room wires habits, let's see how these small, automatic loops become the building blocks of extraordinary success—not through grand gestures, but through daily, deliberate shots.

Most people think success is about grand gestures—quitting your job to chase a dream, running a marathon with no training, or flipping your life upside down overnight. But as we've seen through stories like Alex Ferreira's relentless practice or my own incremental battles on the Snowbird Hill Climb, the path to greatness is paved with small, consistent steps. Habits are those steps.

The filmmaking process mirrors our *Mental Mastery Pyramid* in remarkable ways. Production requires resilience as our foundation, mental strengthening through challenges, mindset control to direct our focus, narrative direction to shape our story, problem-solving to overcome obstacles, achievement systems to reach our goals, a champion's integrated approach, never-quit determination, gratitude for progress, and adaptation to unexpected circumstances. Now, we're adding automation through habits—the production workflows that ensure consistent excellence shot after shot, scene after scene.

In the film world, where I spent my early career, we understand instinctively that a blockbuster isn't created in one take—it's thousands of shots, carefully planned and executed, then stitched together in post-production. Success in any field follows this pattern of small, deliberate actions compounding over time. Back when I was just starting out in the warehouse of a production company, I pitched in on set with small crews, taking on any task to keep things running smoothly. I made it a habit to go the extra mile, like spending late nights researching and testing fake blood concoctions for a big client's gory shot. It wasn't glamorous, but one day on set, that preparation nailed the scene in a single take, saving hours of reshoots and earning me the crew's trust. That trust, and my mantra of no job being too small, eventually opened the door to my first editing gig.

Each micro-shot compounds like frames in a montage, building your blockbuster life—a principle we've seen with the 1% Solution where small improvements add up over time. When I decided to train for my first Ironman, I didn't start with a 140.6-mile race. I started with 25 yards in the pool—barely a lap—because that's all I could manage without gasping for air. But I showed up the next day, and the next, each time adding a little more distance. Those tiny daily wins compounded into crossing the finish line 8 months later.

Habits are particularly powerful for pushing past the *Breakthrough Threshold*—that gap between perceived limits and actual capacity. When behaviors become automatic, they bypass the brain's natural fatigue signals that normally kick in long before you reach your true limits. This explains why I could maintain my training schedule on days when motivation was completely absent—my habits carried me through barriers that conscious willpower could never penetrate.

One small habit that transformed my consistency was keeping a fitness journal, much like the production logs we maintained for film shoots. It sounds simple—recording my workouts, their timings, and durations—but it was a game-changer, similar to the systematic tracking Alex Kopacz used to engineer his Olympic success. Writing them down made them real, tangible, and trackable, echoing the visual tracking systems we discussed earlier about goal achievement.

The beauty of habits is they don't rely on motivation, which is fickle at best. Motivation got me to sign up for the Ironman, but it vanished two weeks into training when my body ached and my mind screamed, "Why are you doing this?" Habits carried me through—those automatic behaviors I'd wired into my day, like laying out my swim gear the night before or setting a non-negotiable time to hit the pool.

A Step-by-Step Guide to Building Good Habits and Breaking Bad Ones

Building habits that stick isn't about brute force—it's about strategic implementation. Drawing on decades of refining my own routines and studying the habits of champions, I've crafted a five-step process that integrates seamlessly with the *Mental Mastery Pyramid* we've been building. Like a production shot list that ensures nothing gets missed, this system delivers results scene by scene, day by day.

Step 1: Start Ridiculously Small (The Micro-Shot)

If your goal is to run a marathon, don't start with five miles—start with putting on your running shoes and stepping outside for one minute. Make it so easy failure becomes impossible. When building my writing habit, I began with just one sentence daily—like filming a single frame instead of a scene. It felt laughable but eliminated the intimidation of a blank page. These small wins create momentum that rewires your brain.

Step 2: Stack New Habits Onto Existing Ones (Scene Transitions)

Your day is already full of automatic behaviors—brushing your teeth, making coffee, checking your phone. Use these as anchors to stack new habits onto, like scene transitions in a film where one action flows naturally into the next. After I brush my teeth each morning, I now spend one minute stretching—a habit I wanted to build to improve my Spartan race recovery. The existing cue (brushing) triggers the new behavior (stretching), and before long, they're inseparable. This echoes the 5-Second Launch Code we discussed earlier, where we program our mornings with intentional thoughts.

Step 3: Remove Friction Between You and the Habit (Set Design)

Environment shapes behavior more than willpower ever will—just like a well-designed film set makes a scene easier to shoot. If I want to hit the gym, I lay out my clothes the night before—shoes by the door, water bottle filled, keys on top. If I want to eat healthier, I keep fruit visible and hide the chips. When I tackled my snacking habit, I stopped buying chips altogether and replaced them with pre-cut veggies in the fridge—easy access for the good, friction for the bad. We'll dive deeper into designing your environment for success in the next chapter, but for now, focus on clearing the set with these simple tweaks.

Step 4: Reward the Behavior Immediately (The "Cut!" Moment)

Your brain loves rewards—it's why the habit loop works. Apply this to your habits. When I finish a writing session, I let myself grab a cup of coffee or listen to a favorite song, creating a small dopamine hit.

This immediate reward system works hand-in-hand with the Three-Win Wake-Up gratitude practice we explored earlier. By celebrating the completion of your habit, you're essentially practicing targeted gratitude—acknowledging your own effort and creating positive emotional associations that reinforce the behavior. This combines the neurological benefits of gratitude with the psychological reinforcement needed for habit formation.

The reward doesn't have to be big, but it needs to be immediate. When breaking my snacking habit, I'd reward a snack-free evening with a few minutes of a favorite podcast—small, but enough to keep me coming back to the new loop. Over time, the habit itself becomes rewarding, but early on, these small dopamine hits keep you engaged.

Step 5: Reframe Your Identity Around the Habit (Character Development)

Goals are great, but identity shifts are better. In filmmaking, the most compelling characters undergo transformations that change who they are at their core. Your habits work the same way. Instead of saying, "I want to run three times a week," say, "I'm a runner." When I started seeing myself as a writer—not just someone writing a book—sitting down to type became less of a chore and more of who I am. When I tackled my weight gain, I shifted from "I need to eat less" to "I'm someone who fuels my body well," a powerful example of narrative rewriting in action.

To break a bad habit, reverse the process: identify the cue (stress triggered my editing procrastination), disrupt the routine (I replaced perfectionist tweaking with a strict time-blocking system), and remove the reward's appeal (I reminded myself how that false sense of productivity led to last-minute panic).

When Your Production Hits Snags: Troubleshooting Your Habit Formation

Even the best directors face production challenges. When (not if) your habit-building efforts hit obstacles, here's how to keep rolling:

If You Miss a Day: Don't scrap the entire production. In filmmaking, we never abandon a project because of one bad take. Simply reset and shoot again tomorrow. This embodies Sam Pedlow's 80/20 system—maintaining discipline in 80% of your habits while allowing 20% flexibility for sustainability. Remember, the continuity of your story matters more than a perfect shooting record.

If Tracking Feels Overwhelming: Simplify your production log. A single check mark on a calendar or a quick note in your phone can be enough. Set a reminder on your phone for one week to log your wins until it feels automatic.

If Motivation Vanishes: Return to your 'why'—the purpose behind your project. On difficult film shoots, we always reconnect with the story we're trying to tell. Write your 'why' on a sticky note and place it where you'll see it daily.

If Progress Seems Slow: Review your dailies—the small wins you've accumulated. Just as directors review footage to see what's working, take time to acknowledge how far you've come. Mark one small win each day on a calendar to see your streak grow visually.

If Resistance Feels Overwhelming: Channel a director's vision—picture the final cut of your goal, visualizing it in vivid detail, and let that image pull you through the tough scenes.

The most successful productions aren't the ones without problems—they're the ones that solve problems creatively and keep the cameras rolling no matter what.

Action Over Intelligence: Why Life Rewards Action, Not Overthinking

I've met brilliant people who never achieve their potential because they're paralyzed by overthinking. They analyze every angle, wait for the perfect moment, and drown in "what-ifs." In film production, we call this being stuck in "development hell"—where great ideas die because they're never actually shot. Meanwhile, the person who takes consistent, imperfect action—however small—keeps moving forward. Life rewards the doers, not the thinkers, a lesson we saw in Yura Min's quick thinking during her Olympic wardrobe malfunction when she had to adapt on the fly.

This became painfully clear later in my production career, when I was still learning the ropes of balancing creativity with deadlines. I was racing against time to finish a project, the deadline looming just hours away. Around midnight, I hit a creative wall—a key element just wouldn't come together. Instead of making a call, I spent hours tinkering with different approaches, second-guessing each one, my coffee growing cold beside me as the editing bay's clock ticked relentlessly forward.

Finally, at 2 a.m., my boss—who was like a mentor—walked in, saw me stuck in a loop of indecision, and said something I'll never forget: "Just finish the damn thing. If it's not right, we'll tweak it later. But right now, you're not working—you're stalling." His words hit like a spotlight in the dark—I was squandering precious time while the event deadline bore down on me. I wrapped it up, my hands shaky but decisive, and sent it off just before dawn.

It's the same lesson I learned on the wrestling mat—where a single thought, "What if he's just as tired as I am?" shifted defeat into victory —or when I pivoted to Chattanooga after the Tahoe Ironman cancellation. The habit of doing—of taking that first step, however small— trumps intelligence or planning when it comes to results.

The Habit of Doing What You Say You Will Do: The Ultimate Self-Accountability

If there's one habit that overrides everything else, it's this: doing what you say you're going to do. It's the bedrock of self-trust, the foundation of every success I've ever achieved. When your words and actions align, you build a confidence that's unshakable—because you know you can count on yourself. It's like directing a scene as scripted—no rewrites, no excuses—just action.

This habit of doing what you say you're going to do perfectly embodies the Earn-It Mindset we explored through Cooper Kupp's journey. Just as Kupp recommits daily to excellence, viewing each day as a fresh opportunity to earn his achievements rather than rest on past accomplishments, the habit of keeping promises to yourself requires that same daily recommitment. Success isn't something you achieve once—it's something you earn anew each day through consistent action.

Years ago, I promised myself I'd run a Spartan race with my son. Life got busy—work piled up, excuses multiplied—but I'd made the commitment out loud, to him and to myself. So I showed up, unprepared and nervous, and we crossed that finish line together. It wasn't pretty, but it was done. That moment didn't just strengthen our bond; it strengthened my belief in my own integrity, much like the gratitude I felt for my family's support at the end of my Ironman journey.

Breaking this habit does the opposite. Every time you say you'll do something and don't, you chip away at your confidence. It's why people who constantly flake on their own goals feel stuck—they've eroded their self-trust. The fix? Start small. Say you'll write one sentence today, and do it. Say you'll walk for five minutes, and go. Each kept promise rebuilds the foundation, brick by brick, echoing the power of micro-wins we celebrated earlier.

Discipline as the Ultimate Self-Love: Ignoring Short-Term Comfort for Long-Term Success

Discipline gets a bad rap—people think it's about deprivation or punishment. But I've come to see discipline as the ultimate act of self-love. It's choosing the version of you five years from now over the version who wants to binge Netflix tonight.

This perspective builds directly on the Deliberate Discomfort practice we explored earlier. When I committed to those daily cold plunges, I wasn't punishing myself—I was honoring my future self.

Each uncomfortable moment represented a declaration: "I respect myself enough to show up, even when it's hard." Discipline isn't saying no to pleasure; it's saying yes to something bigger—the difference between temporary satisfaction and lasting fulfillment.

Your Habit-Building Playbook: Take Action Now

Before moving on, take five minutes to apply this framework to your impossible goal. Quick implementation now will dramatically increase the likelihood you'll follow through later.

First, identify one ridiculously small habit that would move you toward your goal—something so tiny it seems almost laughable. Remember, we're looking for the habit equivalent of that first 25-yard swim, not the full Ironman.

Next, identify an existing routine you can stack this new habit onto. What daily behavior can serve as your trigger? The moment after you brush your teeth, pour your coffee, or arrive at your desk can become the cue that initiates your new habit automatically.

Now, plan to remove friction. List three specific ways you'll make this habit easier to perform—perhaps laying out equipment the night before, setting a reminder, or eliminating a competing distraction. Remember that environment often trumps willpower.

Fourth, decide on your immediate reward. How will you celebrate taking action? Make it small but meaningful—a moment of acknowledgment, a favorite song, or a brief break. This immediate reinforcement wires the habit loop more quickly than delayed gratification.

Finally, reframe your identity around this habit. Complete this statement in your mind: *"I am someone who..."* This identity shift transforms your habit from something you do into someone you are becoming.

Commit to this ONE habit for the next 30 days. Track your progress daily using whatever system works for you—a simple calendar, a digital app, or a notebook. The method matters less than the consistency. Remember, in habit formation, showing up regularly trumps showing up perfectly.

Before You Move On: Your First Scene

In filmmaking, there's a magical moment called "first day of principal photography"—when all the planning, all the pre-production meetings, all the casting sessions finally culminate in someone calling "Action!" for the very first time. It's the moment when a project transforms from an idea into reality. That's what this moment is for you right now.

I still remember the first time I called "Action!" on a tiny student film set—nervous, unprepared, but alive with possibility, just like the first 25-yard pool lap I swam when training for my Ironman. That's what your first habit can feel like—the start of a production that changes everything.

Your life's greatest achievements won't begin with fanfare or perfect conditions. They'll begin with that first, small scene—shot when no one's watching, when doubts are loud, when the path ahead seems unclear. But that first scene changes everything. It's the moment you stop rehearsing life and start directing it.

So call "Action!" on your habit today. Because the key to success isn't willpower. It's habit power. And now, you know how to build it, just as you've learned to build resilience, rewrite narratives, and master uncertainty throughout this journey above the shoulders.

As powerful as these habit systems are, they don't exist in isolation. Next, we'll explore how the people around you—your social environment within the 25-Foot Rule of influence—either reinforce or undermine the habits you're building. The environment you design becomes the stage where your habits perform, either supporting your automation systems or sabotaging them before they take root. This is why the next layer of our *Mental Mastery Pyramid* focuses on creating the optimal social conditions for your habits to thrive.

The director's chair is waiting. It's your production now.

PART IV

SHAPING YOUR LIFE THROUGH MINDSET

CHAPTER 12: THE PEOPLE AROUND YOU DETERMINE YOUR SUCCESS

I waited in the wings before my first public speaking event, pulse quickening as I checked my notes one last time. The audience wasn't particularly large, but as someone more comfortable behind the scenes than in the spotlight, I felt the weight of the moment.

Beside me stood Alex Kopacz—Olympic bobsledder, gold medalist, and a close friend.

He must have sensed my nervousness, because he leaned over and said, *"Remember, the stage is just another mountain. You've climbed bigger ones."*

But what calmed me most wasn't just his words—it was knowing he was going up there with me. That he wouldn't let me fail. That if I stumbled, he'd seamlessly step in. His presence made me feel like I could do anything. That moment crystallized a truth I'd been living: the right people don't just change your mood—they literally rewire your brain.

This chapter builds directly on the mental frameworks you've already strengthened: resilience, cognitive stamina, mindset control, narrative mastery, and the ability to break negative loops.

Now we're taking it one level deeper—into your environment.

Because your social circle doesn't just influence your mood—it shapes your brain. The people around you can either accelerate your growth or sabotage it, right down to the neurological level.

Most people think I'm lucky because my job in sports marketing puts me around elite athletes. They see the events, the gear, the excitement. But they miss the real advantage—it's not the perks of the job; it's that my daily work surrounds me with humans who've pushed beyond what most consider possible. My career has given me the ultimate edge: an inner circle of some of the most determined, disciplined, and successful people on the planet. These athletes don't just perform physically; they've mastered what happens above the shoulders. They treat mental barriers like suggestions, not laws. When that becomes your normal—when excellence is what you're immersed in every day—it fundamentally recalibrates what you believe you can do.

Your brain doesn't care about fairness or good intentions. It's constantly scanning your environment and adapting to whatever dominates it. That process happens whether you're conscious of it or not. Your circle isn't just influencing you; it's programming you, synapse by synapse.

Your Circle Can Make You or Break You

"You couldn't do an Ironman."

Six words casually tossed during a hallway conversation at work. He had no idea those words would transform me—not because they hurt, but because they sparked something. They became the flint that lit a fire that carried me through 140.6 miles of swimming, biking, and running.

But here's what most people miss: While that challenge ignited my journey, it was my inner circle that sustained it. My wife, who never once questioned if I could finish, only how—her unwavering belief in me when I couldn't believe in myself. My son watching me push through that desert race in Abu Dhabi, learning that when your body quits, your mind can still go.

And then there was my cousin's comment when the Lake Tahoe race got canceled by wildfires. She was battling stage-four cancer, yet found the strength to remind me: *"At least you can still do this."*

Those five words pierced straight through my self-pity and completely shifted my perspective. Her courage in the face of real struggle made my setback seem trivial—and gave me the mental reset I needed to pivot to Chattanooga.

The distance between your potential and your reality is often determined by the five people you spend the most time with. They establish your normal. They set your standards. They shape what you believe is possible.

I've had both kinds of relationships—the ones that expanded me and the ones that constrained me. I've noticed how draining it can be to carefully measure your words around people who consistently focus on what might go wrong. And I've experienced the energizing effect of spending time with someone who naturally spots possibilities where others see roadblocks.

The difference isn't just emotional—it's neurological. Negative interactions flood your body with cortisol, the stress hormone that clouds thinking and disrupts sleep. One study showed that even brief exposure to negativity impairs your brain's ability to solve problems by up to 39%. Like a computer virus corrupting your operating system, toxic relationships hijack your mental software, running programs of doubt instead of possibility.

The People Who Prove What's Possible

"You didn't just climb that hill—you owned it. What's next?"

My closest friend's first words after I called him, gasping and vomiting at the summit of Snowbird after finally breaking the 60-minute barrier I'd chased for years. He didn't dwell on the achievement—he immediately pushed me to look beyond it. That's not just friendship; it's the kind of support that transforms achievement into momentum for the next challenge.

The night before I flew out to Chattanooga, doubt settled over me like a heavy fog. That familiar voice of uncertainty kept suggesting I might be in over my head. My wife sat with me at our kitchen table, her hand steady on mine. She didn't try to convince me with logic or dismiss my fears. Instead, she reminded me of every early morning I'd rolled out of bed at 4 AM to train. Every weekend I'd sacrificed. Every milestone I'd already conquered.

"You've already done the hardest part," she said with absolute certainty. "Chattanooga is just the victory lap."

The way she said it—not as encouragement but as simple fact—rewired something in my brain. Even though she couldn't join me on this trip, her confidence became mine, not because she cheered me on, but because she genuinely couldn't see any outcome other than my success. This is what the right people do—they don't make the mountain smaller, they make you a better climber.

Your most substantial growth happens through relationships, not revelations. Information is everywhere, but transformation happens in the space between people who push each other. Find someone who believes in your highest potential, especially when you don't, and you've found something precious. Be that person for someone else, and you've become precious yourself.

The Three Circles That Create Your Reality

Your environment isn't a single relationship—it's a series of three concentric circles, each shaping your mental landscape in distinct ways:

1. Your Professional Circle

This circle dominates your waking hours, flooding your brain with either possibility or limitation. I vividly remember a boss early in my production career who changed everything with one comment. After I'd stayed up all night fixing a botched project someone else had screwed up, he said, "I notice you never bring me problems without solutions." That one line—recognizing a strength I didn't know I had —rewired how I approached every challenge after. One sentence altered my professional identity, not because it was profound, but because it came from someone whose opinion mattered to me.

Your colleagues, mentors, collaborators, and even competitors collectively establish your professional standard—what feels acceptable, what seems possible, and what you consider "normal" effort. This circle includes not just those you work with directly, but also the thought leaders, industry experts, and role models you follow professionally.

2. Your Personal Circle

This circle includes your partner, family members, and closest friends—the people who see you at your most authentic and vulnerable. Their influence runs deepest because these relationships tap into your most fundamental needs for belonging, love, and identity.

My dad's casual comment about sports being "80% above the shoulders" planted a seed that grew into this book's entire philosophy. The people who raised you installed your original mental software. The question is: Are you running updates, or are you still operating on the original programming?

Your partner shapes your daily reality more than anyone else. The person you wake up with either consistently reinforces your boldest vision or subtly undermines it. Most people spend more time researching a car purchase than considering this question about their relationship: Does this person make me more or less of who I'm meant to be?

Throughout this book, you've seen how Olympic aerial skier Ashley Caldwell transformed her setbacks into opportunities.

Her *rebuilding vs. recovering* mindset didn't just impact her career—it seeped into my thinking through our regular interactions.

While most people ask, *"How do I get back to normal?"* after a setback, I started automatically asking, *"How do I use this to come back stronger?"*

Ashley's champion's perspective became my default—not because she lectured me, but because I witnessed her live it day after day.

Her normal became mine—not through pressure, but through proximity.

3. Your Extended Circle

This circle encompasses your broader network of acquaintances, community connections, and digital influences—the content you consume, the social media you follow, and the cultural inputs you absorb daily.

During my Ironman training, I ruthlessly purged my social feeds of anyone who normalized quitting while deliberately filling them with ultramarathoners who made my goals seem modest by comparison. Within weeks, my entire perception shifted—4:00 AM training sessions weren't "impossible"; they were just what athletes like me did.

I created a digital environment that reinforced the mental patterns I was trying to build, understanding that my brain would absorb these influences whether I was conscious of it or not. One ultra-endurance podcast I started listening to daily completely shifted what I considered "normal" training volume, not through any single episode, but through the cumulative effect of hearing these stories regularly. My standards unconsciously recalibrated based on what I consistently exposed myself to.

Every circle is constantly programming what your brain perceives as possible, acceptable, and normal. The question isn't whether this is happening—it's whether you're directing it deliberately or letting it happen by default.

The 25-Foot Rule: Why Proximity Matters So Much

As we discovered earlier, research shows that if you sit within 25 feet of a high performer, your own performance can improve by up to 15%.

But the flip side is ruthless—sit within 25 feet of a low performer, and your performance can drop by up to 30%.

This isn't motivation theory; it's data from a study following over 3,000 employees across multiple companies for five years. Your brain is constantly calibrating to the energy, standards, and output of those around you, whether you realize it or not.

The neurological mechanism behind this is remarkably similar to the mental forge concept we explored in Chapter 2. Just as London's cab drivers developed enlarged hippocampi through their rigorous mental training, your brain physically changes in response to your social environment. The neural pathways that fire when you're around high performers literally strengthen with each exposure, gradually transforming your default patterns of thinking and behavior.

The primary brain structures responsible for this are mirror neurons —specialized brain cells that fire both when you perform an action and when you see someone else perform it. They're why you cringe when someone gets hurt on video, why you instinctively smile when someone smiles at you, and why excellence or mediocrity is contagious.

A Harvard study tracking over 12,000 people for three decades found that if a close friend becomes obese, your likelihood increases by 57% —even if they live miles away. If they quit smoking, your odds of quitting jump by 36%. If they're happy, your happiness rises by 25%. We are neurologically wired to sync with our surroundings.

I felt this during my darkest moment in the Ironman—mile 18 of the marathon, legs shot, stomach revolting, when a complete stranger ran beside me for half a mile, saying nothing but matching my pace. His presence alone kept me from walking. He didn't offer a word of encouragement—he didn't need to. His proximity was power.

The Overthinker's Advantage

If you're an overthinker like me, this environmental influence hits even harder. Our brains process social cues more deeply, making us emotional sponges for the attitudes around us. A casual dismissive comment can send us into a doubt spiral; a word of genuine belief can fuel us for months.

This sensitivity isn't weakness—it's a superpower when channeled right. But it means you have to be even more vigilant about who gets access to your mental space. I've learned to be ruthlessly selective about who I process challenges with. Some people turn problems into threats; others turn them into puzzles. The difference determines whether I walk away energized or depleted.

When preparing for an important team presentation at work, I called one specific friend beforehand—not the one who would say "you'll crush it," but the one who would ask questions that sharpened my thinking. You need different voices for different moments. The key is choosing them deliberately instead of reaching out to whoever's available.

I once had a friend who responded to every achievement with, "Don't get your hopes up," and every setback with, "I told you so." He wasn't malicious—just chronically concerned about disappointment. But his caution became a tax on my ambition, a cognitive friction that slowed every bold move. I started filtering what I shared, saving my biggest goals for people who responded with "How can we make that happen?" instead of "Why would you want to try that?"

Upgrading Your Inner Circle: The Practical Method

So how do you actually build a circle that expands rather than limits you? Here's my battle-tested approach:

1. Do an Unfiltered Circle Audit

List the five people you spend the most time with in each of your three circles (professional, personal, extended). Not who you wish it was—who it actually is. For each person, ask these specific questions:

> After spending time with this person, do I feel more capable or less capable?
>
> Do they raise my energy or drain it?
>
> Do they make me more likely to take action or more likely to hesitate?
>
> Do they respond to challenges with solutions or complaints?
>
> Do they hold me to higher standards or let me off the hook?

During my audit, I realized something uncomfortable—some of the people I enjoyed most were also the ones who normalized settling. Their humor and companionship came with an invisible cost: they made exceptional effort seem unnecessary, even foolish. This wasn't about judging them; it was about understanding their impact on my standards.

2. Strategically Manage Your Exposure

You don't necessarily need to cut people off, but you do need to control dosage. For negative influences you can't eliminate (certain family members, coworkers), create boundaries around time, topics, and energy investment.

Here are specific boundary-setting phrases I've used that preserve relationships while protecting my mental environment:

"I appreciate your concern, but right now I'm looking for strategy, not assessment."

"Let's focus on solutions rather than rehashing the problem."

"I've decided to keep this particular goal private until it's further along."

"I'm trying something new with how I approach challenges—I'm practicing looking for opportunities instead of obstacles."

When I realized a longtime friend consistently undermined my goals with "realistic" warnings, I didn't end the friendship. I just stopped discussing certain topics with him. Our relationship survived but transformed into something that protected my mental environment.

For positive influences, deliberately increase exposure. Schedule regular calls, training sessions, or coffee meetings. Don't wait for chance encounters with people who elevate you—create systems that ensure regular connection.

3. Put Yourself in High-Performance Environments

If your current circle doesn't have enough high performers, change where you spend time. Join groups, classes, or communities where excellence is the norm. I started attending workshops and events far outside my budget, not for the content, but for the people. Being the least accomplished person in the room isn't comfortable, but it's transformative.

The key is consistency over intensity. One weekend mastermind won't rewire your brain—but showing up in growth-minded environments regularly will. It's not about networking; it's about recalibrating your normal.

4. Create Virtual Mentorship

You don't need direct access to world-class performers to benefit from their influence. Books, podcasts, documentaries, and interviews can provide proximity to thinking you want to absorb. I've had "mentors" who don't know I exist—people whose content I consume so regularly that their mindset has shifted mine.

This isn't about information—it's about immersion. Spend the first 15 minutes of your day consuming content from people who embody what you're aiming for. Your brain doesn't distinguish as much as you think between physical and virtual influences.

5. Become the Person You Want to Attract

The fastest way to upgrade your circle? Become the kind of person you want to be around. Be relentlessly positive. Solve problems instead of complaining about them. Celebrate others' wins without qualification. Show up when it counts.

Energy is contagious, but it starts with you. I've watched my circle transform not by seeking new people, but by changing what I bring to every interaction. High performers are drawn to others who match their standards and energy. Become that person, and watch how your circle naturally upgrades.

Your Circle = Your Future

The most significant predictor of where you'll be five years from now isn't your goals, your knowledge, or even your habits. It's the five people you spend the most time with. They are the architects of your future self, the sculptors of your potential, the invisible hand guiding what happens above the shoulders.

When I finally crossed that Ironman finish line in Chattanooga—after the Lake Tahoe cancellation, after the bike crash into some poor guy's mailbox, after fighting through every doubt my mind could generate—it wasn't just my victory. It belonged to everyone who had programmed possibility into my thinking when I couldn't see it myself.

Your life expands or contracts in direct proportion to the belief systems you're surrounded by. Choose wisely, because above the shoulders, your circle becomes your reality.

As we move into our final chapter on lifelong growth, you'll discover how to maintain momentum when others plateau. The environmental design you've just created becomes the foundation for that ongoing expansion—the ecosystem where your potential doesn't just survive but thrives.

Your Next Move: The Circle Audit

Before you move to the next chapter, take five minutes—right now—to assess your circle:

1. Map Your Three Circles: List the most influential people in your professional circle, personal circle, and extended circle.

2. Evaluate Their Impact: For each person, answer: Do they expand or limit what you believe is possible? Do they energize or drain you? Do they make challenges feel solvable or overwhelming?

3. Plan Strategic Adjustments:

• Identify one relationship that needs more boundaries. What specific topic, time limit, or interaction pattern will you adjust this week?

> Choose one relationship to deliberately strengthen. Who consistently makes you better? Schedule a specific time to connect with them in the next seven days.

> Find one new environment where the type of people you want to become naturally gather. Put it on your calendar—not as a someday goal, but as a specific commitment with a date and time.

4. Craft Your Boundary Language: Write down the exact words you'll use to create healthy distance with people who drain your mental energy while maintaining the relationship.

This isn't about judgment or abandonment—it's about deliberate curation of the most powerful external force shaping your internal reality. Because in the end, the people around you aren't just part of your life story—they're co-authors of it. Choose your co-authors with the care your story deserves.

CHAPTER 13: LIFELONG GROWTH—HOW TO KEEP EXPANDING YOUR POTENTIAL

The Moment It All Clicked

"*You're out of your league.*"

Those words weren't spoken—they were written all over the CMO's face as I pitched my marketing ideas after years in production. No marketing degree. No fancy resume. Just a guy who'd spent years filming athletes, convinced he could reimagine how our company used them.

I was sweating through my shirt, watching their skeptical glances, feeling like an imposter with every slide. Then a thought hit me like a freight train. I looked them straight in the eyes and said, "Look, I know I don't have a marketing degree, but I've been telling stories my entire career—and isn't that what marketing is? Telling stories?"

The room shifted. Their body language opened up. That single moment—that mental reframe from "unqualified outsider" to "experienced storyteller"—changed everything.

Once I got the job, I didn't coast. On calls, when someone dropped terms like "VIK" or "IP," I'd nod confidently, then sprint to my office to

Google what the hell they meant. Every gap became a target. Every weakness became an opportunity to get better.

That's what this entire journey has been building toward: mental mastery isn't a destination.

It's a launchpad.

The resilience, the discipline, the mindset control—it all leads to one final truth:

Growth isn't something you do occasionally.

It's who you become permanently.

The Brutal Truth About Comfort

Let me tell you what happened after my first Spartan World Championship in Lake Tahoe. After months of grueling training and crossing that finish line, I experienced something unexpected— emptiness. The goal was gone. For three weeks, I did nothing. No training, no challenges, just Netflix and take-out. My body softened, but worse—my mind dulled. The mental edge I'd spent months sharpening began to rust in real time.

This is what happens to most people. They climb the mountain, plant their flag, and then wonder, "What now?" They plateau. Their skills atrophy. The mental sharpness they worked so hard to develop begins to dull.

Why? Because comfort—the very thing most people chase—is actually your deadliest enemy.

Remember those London cabbies? Their brains physically expanded by learning 25,000 streets. When they stopped challenging themselves, those neural pathways began to weaken. It's the same with anything—your mind follows a simple rule: use it or lose it.

Think back to Thomas Edison's 10,000 failed attempts at the light bulb or James Dyson's 5,126 vacuum prototypes. Their success wasn't just persistence—it was their refusal to get comfortable, their commitment to continuous growth even when conventional wisdom suggested they'd reached their limits.

Sam Pedlow: Growth Beyond Achievement

Remember Sam Pedlow? The beach volleyball pro whose 80/20 system showed us how to balance disciplined training with sustainable practice.

His story continues with a moment that perfectly illustrates what life-long expansion really looks like.

Despite mastering the systems and habits we explored in earlier chapters, Sam faced a defining challenge in Mexico, 2021. After rigorous preparation, leaving his eight-week-old daughter behind, he stood at match point for Olympic qualification—up 19-12.

Then the rain crashed down. Temperature dropped to 16°C.

He lost 22-20, then the next set. Olympic dreams, gone in minutes.

In 2016, a similar near-miss had crushed him. "I was the biggest failure alive," he'd told me, falling into depression for months.

But this time, at 33, something remarkable happened—he laughed and said, "So bad it's funny."

That wasn't defeat. That was evolution.

The systems-focused athlete we met earlier had transformed into something more. He realized volleyball was part of him, but not all of him. The court wasn't his ceiling—it was just one arena for his capabilities.

Today, he works as a physiotherapist, using his elite athlete experience to help patients recover faster. He mentors young players, showing them that "Loss is part of the journey, not the end."

Sam didn't just survive the game—he outgrew it. This is the ultimate expression of the mental mastery we've been building: not just excellence within your domain, but the capacity to evolve beyond it.

The No-BS Growth System

I've spent years studying elite performers, experimenting on myself, and cutting through the bullshit to figure out what actually works. When I first decided to write this book, I made zero progress for years. I'd dabble, jot down ideas, but never truly commit. I wanted to write it badly, but I didn't believe in myself.

Eventually, I stopped overthinking and built a ridiculously simple system that I'm going to share with you now. No 12-step processes. No complicated frameworks. Just three non-negotiable components that form my No-BS Growth System:

1. Pick One Thing

Most people try to improve everything at once, which guarantees they'll improve nothing. Elite performers think differently. They choose one specific skill or capability and obsess over it until mastery.

Each year, I identify one area to transform. When I decided to do an Ironman but couldn't even swim 25 yards without gasping for air, I didn't try to improve everything at once. I focused relentlessly on developing a swim technique that would get me through 2.4 miles of open water.

For this book, I focused specifically on storytelling—not marketing, not platform-building, just the craft of turning my experiences into lessons you could actually use.

What's the ONE capability that would most dramatically improve your impossible goal? Not two, not five—ONE. Write it down right now.

2. Show Up Daily

Growth is simple in theory—merciless in execution. It demands consistency when you're exhausted, unmotivated, and completely alone.

I committed to just 30 minutes of writing each morning, attaching it to my existing coffee ritual. Some days I wrote garbage. Some days I stared at the screen. It didn't matter—what mattered was showing up consistently when motivation was absent.

The minimum effective dose is this: 20 minutes of focused effort on your chosen skill, five days a week.

That's it. Not sexy. Not complicated. Just consistent enough to trigger the compound effect that drives real growth.

Block those 20 minutes right now. Not tomorrow. Now. Put it on your calendar with a specific time and place. This isn't negotiable.

3. Get Ruthless Feedback

Your ego is the enemy of your growth. Most people avoid feedback because it hurts, or they seek it from people who won't tell them the truth.

Elite performers do the opposite—they hunt down the most qualified, brutally honest feedback they can find. They don't want to be told they're great; they want to know exactly where they suck so they can improve.

For this book, I shared early drafts with people who wouldn't spare my feelings—people who would tell me when my stories dragged, my points weren't landing, or my advice was too vague.

Find someone who knows what excellence looks like in your chosen area and who cares enough about your growth to tell you the unfiltered truth. Then listen without defensiveness. This is where real acceleration happens.

Who's your feedback person? Decide now and reach out to them within 24 hours.

That's it. The entire system. Pick one thing. Show up daily. Get ruthless feedback. Everything else is just details.

The Emotional Landscape of Growth

There's something I haven't told you about my book-writing journey. The first time I received unfiltered feedback from a trusted editor, my stomach physically clenched. The manuscript I'd poured hundreds of hours into—the one I thought was pretty damn good—came back bleeding with comments, deletions, and questions about fundamental elements I thought I'd nailed.

For twenty-four hours, I couldn't look at it. Every notification email made me flinch. I circled the document like it was a living thing waiting to attack me. That night, I barely slept, cycling between defensive anger (*"They just don't get what I'm trying to do"*) and crushing doubt (*"Maybe I'm not cut out for this"*).

But something happened on the second day. As I forced myself to read the feedback line by line, the sting began to fade. In its place came something unexpected—a surge of clarity and energy. Every criticism pointed to a specific way I could make the work better. Every question highlighted an opportunity to connect more deeply with readers.

By the third day, I was attacking the manuscript with renewed purpose, slashing unnecessary sections, rebuilding weak arguments, and recrafting stories to hit harder. The work became stronger, clearer, more impactful—not despite the painful feedback, but because of it.

The truth about growth is that it's never emotionally neutral. There's an undeniable pain in seeing your limitations exposed, in confronting how far you still have to go. But there's also an exhilaration that comes from pushing through that discomfort, from feeling yourself becoming more capable in real-time.

Your impossible goal will take you through this same emotional landscape—the vulnerability of beginning, the frustration of plateaus, the sting of honest feedback, and finally, the pure rush of breaking through to new capabilities. This emotional journey isn't separate from the growth process—it's an essential part of it.

The Ripple Effect: Your Growth Changes Everything

There's a dimension to growth that transcends personal achievement —the way it transforms everyone around you.

I still remember a blazing summer day in my backyard. I was training for my next Spartan race, flipping a massive tire end over end across the lawn. My muscles burned, sweat poured down my face, and every fiber screamed to stop. That's when I heard the sliding door slam.

My kids burst into the yard, eyes wide with curiosity. "What are you doing, Dad?" Before I could answer, my youngest was already trying to push the tire, legs churning, face red with effort. The others quickly joined in, laughing and grunting as they struggled against its weight.

What started as my solo training session transformed into a family affair—all of us heaving that monster tire, tumbling, laughing, getting after it together. During a water break, my son asked why I kept going when it looked so hard.

"It's not about nailing it perfectly," I told him. "It's about sticking with the suck. The hard stuff is where the good stuff happens."

I didn't realize the impact of that moment until weeks later, when I caught him struggling with a difficult math problem, muttering to himself, "Stick with the suck, stick with the suck." He wasn't just repeating my words—he was internalizing the mindset.

That day crystallized something powerful: your growth isn't just about you. When you commit to expanding your capabilities—when you demonstrate resilience, embrace challenge, and push beyond comfort—you create ripples that affect everyone in your orbit. Your children, teammates, friends, and colleagues don't just hear what you say about mental strength—they watch how you embody it when things get tough.

This isn't about pressure to be perfect. It's about the profound responsibility and opportunity that comes with understanding that your mental approach to challenge becomes a template for others. When you quit easily, they learn to quit easily. When you persist through difficulty, they learn persistence is possible for them too.

Your impossible goal, approached with the simple system I've shared, becomes more than personal achievement—it becomes a beacon showing others what's possible above the shoulders.

Your Hard Days Strategy

Let's be real—you're going to have days when you don't want to show up. Days when it feels pointless. Days when Netflix and a bag of chips sound way better than pushing through the discomfort of growth.

These Hard Days separate those who actually transform from those who just talk about it. Here's my simple Hard Days Strategy:

1. Commit to Five Minutes

On days when you really don't want to show up, don't try to force a full session. Just commit to five minutes. That's it. Almost always, once you start, you'll continue past five minutes. But even if you don't, you've maintained the most important thing—the habit itself.

2. Remember Your Why

Don't focus on the task; focus on what it represents. When I really didn't want to write, I wouldn't think about the writing itself—I'd think about the people who might benefit from what I had to share. I'd think about proving to myself that I could finish what I started. I'd think about the example I wanted to set for my kids.

What's your deeper why? It's not about the skill itself—it's about what mastering it represents for your life and identity.

3. Track Your Streak

There's something powerful about not breaking a chain of consistent action. Use a simple calendar or app to mark every day you show up. As that chain grows, you'll become increasingly reluctant to break it.

This isn't just psychological—it's neurochemical. Each check mark gives you a small dopamine hit that reinforces the behavior, gradually making it more automatic and less dependent on motivation.

The Transformation: How It Actually Feels

Remember four years ago when I first committed to writing this book? Let me tell you about the day I knew—really knew—that something fundamental had shifted in me.

I was at my desk, deep into what had become a daily writing routine. Words were flowing with an ease that would have seemed impossible months earlier. I had just finished a section, when I realized something startling—I'd been writing for nearly three hours without checking the time, without feeling tired, without once thinking about stopping.

That moment was like stepping through an invisible doorway. On one side was the person who had struggled to write a single page, who doubted every sentence, who couldn't imagine completing even one chapter. On the other side was someone new—a writer who found joy in the process, who saw challenges as puzzles to solve rather than barriers to progress, who knew with bone-deep certainty that the book would be finished.

The change wasn't just in my writing capability. It was in how I saw myself. Tasks that once seemed daunting now felt manageable. Problems that would have triggered doubt now triggered curiosity. The mental muscles I'd developed through consistent practice hadn't just made me a better writer—they'd made me more confident, more resilient, more capable across every domain of my life.

This is what awaits you on the other side of your growth journey. Not just new skills, but a new relationship with challenge itself. Not just achievement, but transformation of your fundamental identity. This is the ultimate promise of living "above the shoulders"—you become someone who no longer recognizes the limitations that once seemed so absolute.

From Impossible to Inevitable

Four years ago, I wrote in my journal: "Write a book that transforms how people understand mental strength." At the time, it seemed impossible. I had no publishing connections, no platform, no idea how to write something people would actually read.

But I applied the system I just shared with you:

I picked ONE thing (storytelling). I showed up DAILY (30 minutes each morning). I got RUTHLESS feedback (from people qualified to give it).

The book you're holding—the one that seemed impossible four years ago—is now real. Not because I'm special or talented, but because I applied these principles consistently, even on the hard days when nothing seemed to work.

Your impossible goal works exactly the same way. It's not a distant fantasy or wishful thinking. It's a future reality waiting to be created through the consistent application of this ridiculously simple system.

Throughout this book, we've explored how life is 90% above the shoulders—how your mind shapes your reality more powerfully than any external circumstance. Elite athletes like Alex Ferreira, Ashley Caldwell, Alex Kopacz, Yura Min, and Sam Pedlow aren't succeeding because they were born with special gifts. They're succeeding because they've mastered what happens above their shoulders, just as you can.

The final truth is this: Your mind isn't just a tool for achieving goals— it's the ultimate determinant of what's possible for you. The same brain that creates limitations can shatter them. The same thoughts that trigger doubt can ignite certainty. The same focus that narrows possibilities can expand them beyond what you currently imagine.

As you close these pages and return to your daily life, remember that you're not just living your story—you're directing it. The mental tools, frameworks, and practices we've explored are your equipment—the camera, lights, and editing software of your personal production.

Your impossible goal isn't a dream. It's a future scene waiting to be shot, its achievement made inevitable by the mind you've been developing throughout these pages.

The camera is rolling. The set is prepared. The script is in your hands.

Above the shoulders, you have everything you need.

Action.

PULL THE TRIGGER: YOUR 90-DAY PLAN

Your impossible goal is staring you down. Not just a vision anymore—a test of who you really are. The mental toolkit isn't theoretical now. It's in your hands, waiting.

Here's what happens next: Most people will nod, close these pages, and do absolutely nothing. They'll say all the right things about resilience and mental mastery, but never break a sweat implementing a single concept. A smaller group will dabble, trying techniques randomly when motivation strikes. Then there's you—or at least, the version of you that refuses to join those ranks. The you that's willing to get uncomfortable, to look foolish, to fail repeatedly in service of something bigger.

I've stood exactly where you are now. That crack of dawn moment before my first Ironman training session, sitting on the edge of my bed at 4:00 AM, heart pounding like a tribal drum in my ears. My mind racing: *Who am I kidding? I can barely swim 25 yards. I'm going to humiliate myself.* My gear bag sitting there, mocking me. My warm bed beckoning me back.

Implementation Is Where Most Break

Let's skip the sugarcoating.

The resilience scorecard, the mental forge, the habit systems—none of it is a magic pill.

They're mental barbells. Waiting for you to grip them with white knuckles and push until failure.

Then push again.

That feeling in your gut right now? That mix of excitement and doubt? It's not weakness—it's the exact sensation that precedes growth. I felt it before every Spartan race, every speaking gig, every time I submitted chapters of this book. That feeling doesn't disappear with success; it becomes the familiar signal that you're pushing edges worth pushing.

Your 90-Day Mental Warfare Plan

No more vague commitments. Here's your battle strategy:

1. Week One: Pick Your Weapon

Choose one technique—*one*, not five.

Maybe it's the *Bite-Sized Wins* approach that got me through that savage desert dune. Or the *Three Deep Breaths Method* that saved me during the manuscript meltdown.

Pick something that hit you in the gut.

Then use it. Daily. Ruthlessly. Without exception.

2. Weeks 2-4: Rewrite Your Mental Script

Pull out the Narrative Rewriting Process. Document the exact phrases your mind uses to sabotage you. The "you're not qualified" loops. The "what if you fail" spirals. Then craft replacement language that's not positive garbage but tactical truth. When I told myself "The manuscript isn't lost; only the words are. The insights remain," it wasn't optimism—it was an accurate reframe that pulled me out of paralysis.

3. Weeks 5-12: Install Never-Quit DNA

This is where most transformations die—in the gap between knowing and doing.

Commit to one ridiculously small daily action using the *1% Solution*.

Sam Pedlow had food poisoning before a crucial match, yet his system still kicked in. That's your target.

Not motivation—*automation*.

Use the *Circle Audit* to create accountability that doesn't let you off the hook when motivation disappears.

The difference between people who transform and those who just talk about it isn't talent or luck. It's the willingness to execute imperfectly rather than plan perfectly.

Your Breakthrough Threshold Awaits

Ninety days from now, you'll hit what Chapter 8 called your *Breakthrough Threshold*—that moment when your brain screams "enough" but you've built the mental framework to recognize it as just the first barrier, not the true limit. Will you push through or pull back?

Imagine standing at your own finish line, gasping for breath like I was in Chattanooga, knowing in your bones that you've shattered what once seemed impossible. That moment isn't waiting for permission or perfect timing. It's already unfolding with every choice you make after reading these words.

I've dragged you through wrestling mats, desert dunes, mailbox crashes, and manuscript disasters. Not for entertainment, but for evidence—proof that what happens above the shoulders determines everything that follows.

That impossible goal you wrote down in the Introduction? It's not a dream. It's your next reality, waiting for you to step up and claim it.

The mental weapons are loaded. The target is clear.

Pull the trigger.

INDEX

Mental Mastery Tools & Techniques

90% Above the Shoulders Principle – intro, 29, 112, 160

Bite-Sized Wins – 11–12, 20, 162-163

Breakthrough Threshold – 145–146, 162, 239

Friend's 90-Day Birthday Dinner Challenge – 106–109

Gratitude Cascade – 169–174

Mental Mastery Pyramid – intro, 17-19, 138, 200

Pause & Pivot – 46-47, 56, 81, 186, 193

Pre-Decision Technique – 13–15, 37

Reframing Negative Thoughts – 58–61, Chapter 5

Three Deep Breaths Method – 62-63, 70-75, 113

Visualization (Mental Movie Method) – 43, 102–103, 120

The power of "YET" – 38-39, 117

Metaphors & Personal Case Studies

Abu Dhabi Spartan Beast ("Hill of Horrors") – 8–12

Charlotte Move & Hotel Breakdown – 181–182

Ironman Journey – 16, 141-143, 153-157

Manuscript Loss – 78-82

Moving Day Crisis (friend's apartment) – 42-44

Short Film Production Crisis – 100

Snowbird Hill Climb – 143-144, 198

Tire-Flipping with Son (legacy moment) – 230

Utah Winter Reframe (snow & skiing) – 87-89

Wakesurfing 360 Attempt – 37–39

Athlete Spotlights

Alex Ferreira (freestyle skier) – 112–123

Alex Kopacz (bobsledder) – 113, 123-140

Ashley Caldwell (aerial skier) – 64-66, 104-105, 171

Sam Pedlow (beach volleyball) – 98, 134, 226-227

Yura Min (ice dancer) – 191-192

Scientific Case Studies & Research Highlights

London Cabbies & Neuroplasticity – 25–28

Housekeepers Exercise Study – 39–40

Gratitude fMRI Study (UCLA) – 170–171

Central Governor Theory (Timothy Noakes) – 146

Key Phrases & Concepts

Deliberate Discomfort – 44-46, 56, 185, 205

Growth Mindset vs. Fixed Mindset – 38-39

Mental Anchors – 14-15

Narrative Control – Chapter 4

Resilience Scorecard – 17–20, 31

Systems over Motivation – 97

Visualization Science – 102–103, 109, 119-120, 137, 140

Final Challenge

Pull the Trigger (90-Day Challenge) – 237–240

ABOUT THE AUTHOR

Jason Nacey was born in Deadwood, South Dakota, and raised in Salt Lake City, Utah. Deadwood remains a cherished connection to his roots—a place where childhood adventures in the surrounding mountains instilled a lasting appreciation for exploration and pushing boundaries.

Described as innovative, sociable, supportive, and diplomatic, Jason naturally excels at bringing people together and inspiring them toward greater achievements. His openness to new experiences and ability to adapt creatively have been foundational in both his career and personal endeavors.

Jason is an all-or-nothing person. When something captures his interest, he dives in completely. He has never been one to dabble. This passionate intensity has shaped his journey, from award-winning filmmaking and international video production to leading athlete and sponsorship programs in sports marketing.

Jason lives by the mantra, Nobody else is coming to solve your problems. This philosophy, developed during his youth when resources were limited but creativity abundant, drives his belief that success is 90% above the shoulders. He proved this firsthand when, after someone doubted his ability to finish an Ironman triathlon, he signed up immediately—despite initially struggling to swim even a short distance. His resilience carried him through the Ironman, two Spartan World Championships, and some of North America's most challenging mountain climbs.

Despite his sociable nature, Jason openly acknowledges his fear of public speaking, a barrier he continuously conquers by practicing the resilience techniques detailed in this book. What looks like natural confidence often isn't—it's about showing up despite the fear.

For years, Jason resisted writing this book, telling himself he wasn't a writer and had no business discussing mindset without formal credentials. The book kept calling to him, and he kept ignoring it. Then one day he realized he was breaking his own rule—tackling hard challenges is central to who he is. This book became his own test case in controlling narrative and mindset. Today, Jason lives in North Carolina with his wife and their four children, where he continues refining these principles of mental toughness. His journey —including the creation of this book—proves that the gap between impossible and inevitable is much shorter than most realize, and exists primarily above the shoulders.

X x.com/DangerNacey

instagram.com/DangerNacey

linkedin.com/in/jason-nacey

www.ingramcontent.com/pod-product-compliance
Lightning Source LLC
Chambersburg PA
CBHW061610120626
46550CB00004B/1677